The DiNuzzo
Middle-Market Family Office™
Breakthrough

Praise for

THE DiNuzzo
MIDDLE-MARKET FAMILY OFFICE™
BREAKTHROUGH

Increasingly personalized wealth management—in which experienced financial advisors customize portfolios and leverage new technologies to optimize client experiences—is a trend with staying power. In *The DiNuzzo Middle-Market Family Office™ Breakthrough*, advisor P. J. DiNuzzo presents a compelling approach for high income earners and business owners and families with $10 million+ in net worth who are seeking the kind of comprehensive, sophisticated advice typically only seen in family offices. Guided by decades of experience as an advisor to middle-market businesses and their owners, DiNuzzo explains in easy-to-understand language how his strategies thoughtfully address this often-underserved demographic and help them advance their financial goals with peace of mind.

—**Dave Butler**, Chief Executive Officer, Dimensional Fund Advisors

If you are a successful privately held business owner, you need to pay close attention to the structure described by Private Wealth Expert, P. J. DiNuzzo in *The DiNuzzo Middle-Market Family Office™ Breakthrough*. From improving your business to achieving greater physical, mental, and emotional health, P. J. DiNuzzo and his revolutionary Middle-Market Family Office have you covered.

—**Bradley J. Franc**, CEO and Founder of The Succession Coach, LLC

P.J. DiNuzzo's new book addresses a large and important segment of wealth management often lost between the "products" available at the lower end of the retail wealth management market and the high-touch, expensive services catering to multi-generational ultra-high-net-worth families. The thoughtful ideas laid out here will accelerate the democratization of sophisticated family office needs using an integrated, tailored approach.

—**William Haney**, Chair, Enhesa

I have known P. J. DiNuzzo for more than 20 years. In addition to being among the country's elite advisers, P. J. is also one of the finest people I have ever met. He is genuine, he truly cares about his colleagues and clients, and his work ethic is unsurpassed. In *The DiNuzzo Middle-Market Family Office*™ *Breakthrough*, P. J. shares the knowledge that has helped him help so many individuals and families for so many years.

—**Thomas D. Giachetti, Esq**., Chairman, Investment Management Practice Group, Stark & Stark, Attorneys at Law

It is the wise person who understands that there is no joy, peace, or security without health. P.J. DiNuzzo has made it part of his mission to learn how to support good health and mental acuity through both simple habits and advanced biohacking technologies. In this wonderful book, he shares valuable insights to help others optimize their potential in every way for a prosperous, balanced, and healthy life.

—**Amy Gardner**, Director of Education, LightStim

P. J. knocks it out of the park with his latest book, *The DiNuzzo Middle-Market Family Office*™ *Breakthrough*. His holistic approach to finance with a particular emphasis on physical and mental health is quite unique to the industry and further proof that an ounce of prevention is worth a pound of cure.

—**Mark Anthony Duca**, MD FACP, UPMC Executive Health Program

THE DiNUZZO
MIDDLE-MARKET
FAMILY OFFICE™
BREAKTHROUGH

Creating Strategic Tax, Risk,
Cash-Flow, and Lifestyle *Options*
for Successful Privately-Held
Business Owners and
Affluent Families

P.J. DiNUZZO

NEW YORK

LONDON • NASHVILLE • MELBOURNE • VANCOUVER

The DiNuzzo MIDDLE-MARKET FAMILY OFFICE™ BREAKTHROUGH

Creating Strategic Tax, Risk, Cash-Flow, and Lifestyle *Options* for Successful Privately-Held Business Owners and Affluent Families

Published in New York, New York, by Morgan James Publishing. Morgan James is a trademark of Morgan James, LLC. www.MorganJamesPublishing.com

Patrick J. DiNuzzo, CPA, PFS™, MBA, MSTx is the Founder, President, and Lead Consultant at DiNuzzo Middle-Market Family OfficeTM ("DMMFO") and DiNuzzo Wealth Management ("DWM"), an investment adviser registered with the United States Securities and Exchange Commission, located in Beaver, PA and Pittsburgh.

Proudly distributed by Ingram Publisher Services.

Morgan James BOGO™

A FREE ebook edition is available for you or a friend with the purchase of this print book.

CLEARLY SIGN YOUR NAME ABOVE

Instructions to claim your free ebook edition:
1. Visit MorganJamesBOGO.com
2. Sign your name CLEARLY in the space above
3. Complete the form and submit a photo of this entire page
4. You or your friend can download the ebook to your preferred device

ISBN 9781631958335 paperback
ISBN 9781631958359 ebook
Library of Congress Control Number:
2021950751

Cover Design by:
Christopher Kirk
www.GFSstudio.com

Interior Design by:
Chris Treccani
www.3dogcreative.net

Morgan James is a proud partner of Habitat for Humanity Peninsula and Greater Williamsburg. Partners in building since 2006.

Get involved today! Visit MorganJamesPublishing.com/giving-back

This Book Is Dedicated To

Pasquale (Patsy) and Rose
Joe and Anna
Natale (Ned) and Phyllis
Nick and Renee
Mike, Jessica, and Estelle
Patsy, Michaela, Lucca, and Pasquale
Renee, Avery, and Danica
Mark and Jackie
Ashley and Sam

Thank you for your faith, family, hard work, loyalty, authenticity, genuineness, gratitude, appreciation, heritage, tradition, legacy, guidance, wisdom, time, patience, passion, understanding, support, and listening. If you weren't you, I could never be me.

I love all of you and am forever IN Gratitude™ for the immeasurable gifts you have provided me during my life.

Table of Contents

Acknowledgments

My book, *The DiNuzzo Middle-Market Family Office™ Breakthrough* could not have been written without the contributions and input over my lifetime of many family members, team members, individuals, organizations, and the Dimensional Fund Advisors (DFA) team and research department.

Special thanks to my advisory team and their areas of expertise: Mark S. DiNuzzo, Executive Committee Member, Executive VP, CFP, AIF, MBA, Retirement Planning/Risk Management, Wealth Advisor; Michael V. DiNuzzo, Executive Committee Member, SR. VP, CFP, CHFC, MSFS, AIF, Retirement Planning/Risk Management, Wealth Advisor; Carl J. Hartman, Senior VP, Senior Investment Officer, CHFC, AIF, Retirement Planning/Investment Management, Wealth Advisor; Jacob R. Potts, Management Team Leader, VP, CFP, CHFC, AIF, Portfolio Management Trade Team Leader, Wealth Advisor; Robert F. Graham, VP, AIF, MBA, VP Retirement Planning, Wealth Advisor; Leslie D. Taylor-Neumann, Management Team, VP, Wealth Planning Team Leader, AIF, Wealth Advisor; Jennifer B. Reddinger, Management Team, VP, EA, CFP, AIF, Tax and Wealth Advisor; and Ken McDaniel, EA, AIF, Tax Advisor.

Additional special thanks to my fellow team members in our operations department: Jackie DiNuzzo, Executive Committee Member, Compliance Officer/HR Manager; Lisa Faulkner, Senior Client Service Specialist; Terri Tepsic, Executive Administrative Assistant/Marketing Manager; Mikey Ronacher, Client Performance Team Leader; Brooke McMaster, Management Team, Senior Client Service Specialist; Cliff

Smith, IT Director; Ken Aikens, Client Service; Jeff Buckley, Client Service Specialist; Courtney Smith, Client Service Specialist; Renee Foody, Administrative Assistant; Denise Lyons, Bookkeeping Manager; Nick DiNuzzo, Video/Internet Manager; Rose Dessler, Compliance Officer/HR Manager; and the Matriarch of our family, Phyllis Nutz (DiNuzzo), Client Service (Emeritus).

Attorneys: Brad Franc, Ed Renn, C.J. Jacques, Cori Siri, Mary Jane Jacques, and Tom Giachetti.

Certified Public Accountants (CPAs): Ned Conley and Ken Herrmann.

Risk Management Specialists: Clay Saftner.

Wealth Advisors/Financial Advisors: Patsy DiNuzzo, Michael Kitces, and Ross Levin.

Consultants: Nick Pavlidis, Russ Alan Prince, Matt Lynch, Marty Miller, and Dr. Joseph Bosiljevac.

Professors: Gene Fama Sr., Nobel Laureate; Kenneth French; Ed Lazear (deceased); Robert Novy-Marx, Myron Scholes, Nobel Laureate, Merton Miller, Nobel Laureate (deceased), and Harry Markowitz, Nobel Laureate.

Dimensional Fund Advisors (DFA): David Booth, Rex Sinquefield, James L. Davis, Weston Wellington, Dave Plecha, Dan Wheeler (retired), Dave Butler, Gerard O'Reilly, Joel Hefner, Mike McCann, John Wilson, Daniel Essman, Jewell Ward, John "Mac" McQuown, and Marlena Lee.

Companies/Organizations: Dimensional Fund Advisors (DFA), TD Ameritrade Institutional, Fidelity Investments Institutional, and Charles Schwab and Co. Institutional, AICPA, PICPA, NATP.

Thank you to the experts, centers of influence, and other key specialists who shared their wisdom and expertise about our work together changing the lives of many clients and their family members: Russ Alan Prince, Ed Renn, Clay Saftner, Wes Sierk, Frank Seneco, Melissa Bizyak, Peter Sasaki, Brad Franc, Dr. Mark Duca, Dr. Dan Carlin, Peter Wasowski, and Amy Gardner.

And finally, thank you Catherine Turner for your attention to detail in helping me prepare this manuscript for publishing, and to my publisher, Morgan James Publishing, for your continued support behind the scenes to help me share *The DiNuzzo Middle-Market Family Office™ Breakthrough* with successful middle-market closely held business owners and affluent families around the world.

Foreword

More personal and business wealth exists in the world today than ever before, as privately held business owners creatively grow their companies. For example, many of them are using the Internet to reach more customers, run their businesses more efficiently, and expand their operations.

That growth has fueled a sharp rise in the income and net worth of privately held business owners. However, it also has often left them vulnerable to a range of professionals that are less than exceptional. As a result, many privately held business owners are not being served well.

Although the vast majority of Wealth Advisors mean no harm, their successful private business owner clients are, in fact, losing out. Their wealth might be growing, but that growth can mask the full picture because they are being underserved and, even worse, are potentially vulnerable in a number of important areas of their business and personal lives, including risk management, tax planning, business valuation, personal health optimization, and more.

Indeed, state-of-the-art wealth management is only one piece of the puzzle that accomplished business owners need to put together to optimize their business and personal lives. But many of them are working with professionals who don't have the knowledge, expertise, and tools to provide the solutions necessary to optimize important life goals, effectively address health concerns, deal with family dynamics, build a significant legacy, achieve their charitable objectives, and other wants and needs of successful business owners and their companies.

Years ago, being served in that capacity was only an option for ultra-wealthy families worth somewhere in the area of $500 million or more. And, frankly, those families were only able to receive that level of care by using their considerable wealth to form a Single Family Office that employed a team of professionals to work for them full-time.

While the Single Family Office model works amazingly well for the ultra-wealthy, it *only* works well for the ultra-wealthy. They have both the complexity and velocity of need to justify the cost of employing a team of full-time professionals to manage key aspects of their business, personal, philanthropic, and investment affairs.

As you might imagine, hiring a team of high-end professionals to work as a well-coordinated team available exclusively to serve one family doesn't come cheap. It can take a lot of money to justify the cost of operating a Single Family Office. If you don't have both the complexity and the velocity of needs, a Single Family Office is not likely to be the best way to go. That's why only the ultra-wealthy have used Single Family Offices.

But what about the people who have the same *needs* and *wants* as the ultra-wealthy but not the same velocity? What if you could significantly benefit from many of the same services, solutions, and level of care, but you just don't need your team of specialists to work exclusively with you on a full-time basis? Where could you get the same high-quality expertise and level of care and service if you were worth somewhere south of $100 million?

Until recently, you didn't have many options. You could conceivably engage a group of lawyers, accountants and other tax advisors, business advisors, and other professionals on a project-by-project basis, but it would be a lot of work. Even then, to get the best outcomes, you would need to coordinate all these specialists. You would need to find each professional on your own. You would need to know what to ask each professional and what to tell each professional about each other. And you would likely build a piecemeal wealth plan, at best. In reality, you will probably end up with a lot of professionals in many ways in over their heads and working beyond their capabilities. In those cases, you, as the client, suffer.

First, you often miss out on opportunities to achieve your bigger business, family, or philanthropy goals because you don't have the level of care and sophistication necessary to help you achieve those goals. Second, you often end up exposed to unnecessary risks as a result of dangerous gaps in your planning that less sophisticated professionals don't even recognize. Third, you end up having to take time and attention away from what you do best: concentrating on building your business and leading your family.

Today, a small percentage of very clever Private Wealth Advisors have utilized advances in technology and increased their ability to collaborate and efficiently access information and resources to provide successful private businesses and their owners with the same level of care and expertise usually restricted to the ultra-wealthy because of their Single Family Offices through what's referred to in the industry as a *Middle-Market Family Office.*

Using a core, well-coordinated team of internal experts augmented by a truly national and international network of specialists, P. J.'s DiNuzzo Middle-Market Family Office™, or DMMFO, treats your family just like Single Family Office professionals treat the ultra-wealthy families they serve. As one of the few Private Wealth Advisors in the country with the experience, expertise, extensive network of leading professionals, and desire to operate using a truly client-centered approach, P. J. DiNuzzo gets to know you and your business, personal, family, and other goals and concerns before he ever presents you with a single possibility or recommendation.

Only after he gets to know you and deeply understands your goals and concerns does he, and his team, provide you with options to optimize your business, family, and philanthropic life. Once you understand all of your options and the advantages and disadvantages of each, they ask you to do what you do best: make the decision that you believe is best for you, your business, and your family.

P. J. DiNuzzo and his cohesive, well-coordinated team of specialists at the DMMFO are consultants, not salespeople. They work closely with you to discover all your interests and then provide you with viable solutions to achieve them. Unlike the salespeople/professionals, P. J. has a panoply of strategies and tools available to him and never pushes you into any single option. Salespeople, on the other hand, feel they may have only one opportunity to "pitch" you, so they are going to "go for it" with the goal of convincing you that their primary product is the only possible solution for you. That is the opposite of discovery. Frankly, it's manipulative.

Over the rest of *The DiNuzzo Middle-Market Family Office™ Breakthrough*, you will get to experience how the DMMFO works to help people just like you achieve the same level of care and many of the solutions once reserved only for the ultra-wealthy. P. J. DiNuzzo will share stories from some of the experts on his team of specialists who work under his direction to serve clients just like you. These stories each followed the same pattern, starting with a detailed process of discovery and coordination among P. J., his cohesive team of specialists, and, in some cases, additional specialists from his extended network of professionals who help address needs that don't come up as often as others.

As you read through this book, watch for that pattern of discovery, specialist coordination, and presenting the client with options. That's what makes the DMMFO so uncommon in the private wealth industry today. That's what makes this all work so well. That's what separates consultants like P. J. from the vast majority of "pretenders" in the wealth management world.

What P. J. does in this book mimics what he does for successful business owners (and some other affluent families). He brings together and coordinates a team of experts to give his clients solutions backed by a level of service once only available to the ultra-wealthy. In his book, he does the same, using his expertise to bring together experts that demonstrate the care you can receive in a Middle-Market Family Office setting. That's what makes the model work. Without P. J.'s understanding the interests of his clients and then bringing the right specialists together to serve each client's unique situation, the DMMFO model wouldn't work. And that really hits at the core of what the DMMFO is all about: you. Listening to you. Understanding you. And having the structure, cohesive team of specialists, tools, extensive resources, and expertise to help you achieve what's important to you. No sales pitch. No steering you to one choice. No competing interests. No conflicts. Just a well-coordinated team of exceptional experts all dedicated to helping you achieve the business, family, philanthropy, and future you want.

By the end, I'm confident you will understand exactly why the DMMFO is different and how it can help you too.

—Russ Alan Prince

Introduction:

The Challenges with the Status Quo and the Lackluster Existing and Traditional Solutions

In the late 19ᵗʰ century, John D. Rockefeller established what would soon become the blueprint for how a great many ultra-wealthy families managed their fortunes, family interests, and several aspects of their business and personal lives. Rockefeller hired a team of professionals, later referred to as the Rockefeller Family Office, to work full-time managing Rockefeller and his family's legal, tax, investment, business, and personal affairs.

This model of employing full-time professionals to cater to the family's every need created several advantages for Rockefeller and his family.

For example, as employees, the professionals owed the Rockefellers complete loyalty and the highest duties of care. The relationship created duties between the professionals and the Rockefellers that working with an independent insurance or tax advisor did not establish.

Additionally, unlike independent professionals whose continued employment depended on serving their own interests or the interests of their employer, family office professionals' continued employment depended on their ability to help the family achieve their goals and address their concerns. Thus, each professional was completely aligned with the interests of the family.

Moreover, with the sheer complexity and volume of the Rockefellers' world, working with outside professionals and advisors who split their time and focus among hundreds of other clients was not practical. They needed their legal, tax, and business professionals to be working together in lockstep to ensure every piece of their business and personal lives worked in complete unison.

The Single Family Office and Two Classes of Wealth

While the Single Family Office model worked well for the Rockefellers and continues to be extremely effective for a growing number of ultra-wealthy families, it is comparatively expensive to put together. Even moderately wealthy families couldn't afford to hire a team of specialists full-time. That reality created a sharp contrast between how the ultra-wealthy and even moderately wealthy families and business owners have been served for the past 150 years. The ultra-wealthy had a team of professionals at their beck and call, virtually 24 hours a day, 7 days a week. These professionals worked together seamlessly to ensure every move one professional made worked not only in a vacuum but in the context of the other family interests.

Contrast that with how even moderately wealthy families have managed their affairs. Families worth between $10 million and $100 million were managing complex business, financial, and family dynamics on their own while simultaneously trying to grow their core business. Even those who were served by Wealth Advisors, lawyers, and accountants pieced together the other elements of a well-rounded business, family, philanthropy, and wealth management plan together on their own.

Common Pitfalls with the Piecemeal Approach

When successful business owners and wealthy families are forced to manage their own affairs in a piecemeal manner, it creates several now-avoidable problems.

For example, they often end up exposed to salespeople in professional clothing. These professionals come to each meeting ready to pitch their product or service no matter what. This is often easily evident with commissioned salespeople for companies whose livelihood depends on closing sales. In one common example, a business owner sits in a meeting with a professional from an insurance company not knowing that the professional will propose the same "solution" no matter what problem the client tells them they want to solve. Looking for an investment vehicle? They will pitch their life insurance product as a way to accumulate assets. Looking for a retirement plan? They will pitch the same life product. Risk management? Estate planning? Tax planning? You guessed it. The same life insurance product. It doesn't matter what you need, you're getting sold the same life insurance product.

I'm not picking on the insurance industry. Life insurance often plays an important role in a well-rounded wealth plan, and these types of salespeople exist in all the disciplines. But insurance is just one of a great number of options available to successful business owners, and I've never met a goal or concern that could only be addressed by a single product. In fact, I typically find multiple options that could work, each with pros and cons.

Another common problem that successful business owners and wealthy families face is when they are being served by professionals who don't have the necessary experience or specialization to properly care for them.

This happens frequently when the clients' affairs are still being led by the same professional or professionals who served them decades earlier when they were just starting to build their wealth. In some of these instances, the professionals are doing their best to serve their clients. While they may be trusted, they are typically not competent at this level of complexity—they just don't have the experience or sophistication needed. They can still often play a role in the families' affairs moving forward, but their lack of experience and sophistication is hurting their clients. This setup often exposes their clients to dangerous gaps and causes them to miss out on tremendous opportunities to increase their entity value, minimize their tax burden, protect their assets, improve their cash flow, manage complex family dynamics (such as children or second marriages), maximize philanthropy, or achieve other important business or personal objectives.

The ultra-wealthy who benefit from high-performing single and multi-family offices never experience sales pitches from professionals. Their team of specialists knows their goals and affairs in great detail. As new needs arise, their team members ask open-ended questions about their business, personal, and legacy goals as well as their pressing concerns.

Why even after so many years do full-time leading professionals continue to work in this way? For many reasons. For one, needs and desires change over time. Worldviews, family dynamics, health concerns, and many other factors cause goals to evolve. Thus, even the top, most-experienced professionals never assume they always know what a client wants. Additionally, with so many options available to serve their clients, the more they understand their clients' specific and present desires, fears, and motivations, the better they will be able to identify the right options.

A Tale of Two Similarly Situated Families

To appreciate the benefit that my discovery process provides, consider two clients who both want to retire with $500,000 per year in safe income, for example. One is naturally risk averse. They have trouble sleeping when the stock market drops or when tax laws change. The other isn't as affected by volatility in the stock market or changing tax laws. They care more about putting together a plan their spouse can easily understand. The "salesperson/professional" would treat both of those clients pretty much the same. They would explain to the first why their product is the best solution for them and, if the client asked, would describe it as safe and stable. They would explain to the second why their product is the best and, again only if asked, would describe it as simple for anyone to understand.

A true Private Wealth Advisor would respond much differently to each client. They would work to understand each client's full circumstances. They would hardly ever suggest a solution in the initial meeting about the topic, instead taking some time to identify multiple options that can help the client achieve their goal in a way that's consistent with the client's personality and their family's needs. Where possible, they would present multiple options to the client, along with the pros and cons of each. They would also likely invite the client to include their spouse or partner, other key family members, and other professionals in the conversations. In fact, if the clients are both married, the Private Wealth Advisor might encourage the clients to involve their spouses in all meetings so they can present options that best fit the couples' overall goals and personality types. When it comes time to present the options, they would present all options along with the pros and cons of each to help the client choose the option they like best. The professionals do all the work, but the client is always in control and will make all the decisions.

Which experience would you prefer? If you're like many successful business owners, you would prefer the family office experience. You know the feeling of being constantly sold to from salespeople posing as professional advisors. You also likely know the feeling of trying to juggle running a business with managing personal, family, and other important goals while addressing key concerns. And you likely know the frustration of being stressed out by not knowing exactly where you stand when it comes to achieving your goals or better managing life's issues. Do you have enough? Are you missing out on opportunities that will allow you to achieve important business, personal, family, or philanthropic goals? Are you adequately protected from business, legal, health, or financial risks?

Unfortunately, until now that experience was once reserved only for the ultra-wealthy.

Taking You Behind the Curtain

Having managed wealth for successful business owners and wealthy families as a Wealth Advisor since 1989, I have seen what happens when clients become subject to piecemeal planning or either self-centered or unsophisticated advisors. I have led thousands of discovery consultations and financial stress tests and discovered dangerous gaps that have left people exposed to extraordinary losses, liabilities, and lawsuits. And I have uncovered countless missed opportunities that prevented clients from living their best lives or achieving their business, financial, philanthropy, and personal goals. In fact, I can't think of a single successful business owner or wealthy family who has not come to us with at least one dangerous gap or significant missed opportunity since I opened my DiNuzzo Middle-Market Family Office™, which I will talk about in more detail later in my book (DMMFO).

For the rest of my book, I'm going to share with you exactly how a very small percentage of Private Wealth Advisors and I have used technology, hyperspecialization, and a new model of professional service to bring the same experience to successful business owners and wealthy families that was once enjoyed only if your last name were Gates, Rockefeller, Buffett, Bezos, or a handful of other equally wealthy families through what I call a *Middle-Market Family Office.*

I will show you how the DMMFO delivers value to clients just like you. I'll also bring you behind the scenes of the DMMFO to show you the inner workings of how my model can help successful families get the same business, life, legacy, health, and other benefits using a model that only rewards us when my team and I achieve tremendous value for you.

I wrote my book just like I run my DMMFO, inviting members of my core team and extended network of specialists to join me in sharing their wealth of knowledge and experience with you. I describe for you some of the common gaps and opportunities they find in their areas of focus when conducting a discovery process with a successful business owner or wealthy family. I asked each of them to share examples based on actual stories from clients we have served to demonstrate the difference in value between the DMMFO and what many business owners and wealthy families have dealt with.

In writing my book, the goal is not just for you to *learn* about the DMMFO and how I work so you can consider whether working with me would be a good fit for you. The goal is for you to *experience* what it is like to work with the DMMFO so you can *feel* the difference between the typical approach and the DMMFO way.

Only then can you make a truly informed decision about the best way to manage your business and family affairs moving forward in order to truly Discover… Create… and *Live* Your Best-Life™!

PART 1:

———

How Single Family Offices Have Served Ultra-Wealthy Business Owners for Decades

———

Chapter 1

How Ultra-Wealthy Business Owners Use Single Family Offices

When many business owners think about achieving extraordinary success, the first things that come to mind are all the positive effects that level of success brings. From building a better life to making life better for the next generation to making a positive impact through philanthropy, they know that wealth opens the door for incredible possibilities.

Once these business owners finally achieve high levels of success and wealth, however, they are often surprised by the many challenges that arise. Wealth, for instance, can attract requests for money from family, friends, and strangers. It certainly attracts salespeople and scammers. And it can also attract people looking to steal from or even physically harm family members.

Effectively navigating so many opportunities and challenges on top of running such a successful business would be impossible. To start, many of these issues are challenging for the average professionals to identify and address. Many accountants, attorneys, and other professionals don't even know what questions to ask to help successful middle-market business owner clients navigate more sophisticated issues. Thus, you can't reasonably expect a business owner to be able to anticipate and address the multitude of opportunities and concerns that come up across various areas of specialty on top of running their business.

That's why the ultra-wealthy establish Single Family Offices to optimize the family's business, family, philanthropy, and future.

Why Only the Ultra-Wealthy Can Establish Single Family Offices

When business owners hit certain levels of wealth, the time and attention needed to truly optimize their life and protect them and their family members becomes equivalent to operating a full-time business. Their legal needs pile up. Their accounting becomes so nuanced that simple strategies can cost or save millions of dollars in tax obligations. Demands on the family's time become overwhelming, especially when such a significant business continues to grow. The list goes on.

At some point—often somewhere between $250 million and $500 million of net worth—it becomes cost-effective to hire a team of specialists to serve the family on a full-time basis. The family would employ a core team of specialists whose sole responsibility is to get to know the family's needs and goals and help them achieve them. It would generally include a variety of professionals, as well as administrative support. And when something comes up that needs an outside specialist, the Private Wealth Advisor would handle finding, negotiating, and working with the right specialists to achieve the best possible result for the family.

If that sounds costly, it's because it usually is. The professionals who have the level of sophistication needed to identify and address issues for the ultra-wealthy command high salaries and benefits. It can easily cost millions of dollars a year to operate a family office that can adequately serve an ultra-wealthy family on a full-time basis. That's why it generally requires a family to achieve somewhere between $250 million and $500 million in net worth before the additional value created by a family office makes financial sense.

How Single Family Offices Benefit the Ultra-Wealthy

Some of the most recognizable benefits of Single Family Offices include optimizing the family's financial and legal worlds, such as reducing risk, improving cash flow, increasing investment returns, and addressing legal issues.

Those are far from the only benefits of a Single Family Office, however. A Single Family Office handles every detail of the family's life. Simply put, if the family wants or needs something, the Single Family Office acts as a catalyst to get it. Here is a list of just some of the other ways Single Family Offices help the ultra-wealthy:

- Providing investment management expertise aligned with the long-term goals and concerns of the family
- Evaluating *all* legally valid ways to mitigate taxes on a corporate and personal level
- Providing extensive administrative support from ensuring all financial statements are up to date and accurate to paying and tracking all expenses
- Coordinating concierge medical care
- Coordinating security for family members at home and while traveling including protecting them from Internet criminals
- Structuring and managing the family's wealth as well as working with later generations to build a family dynasty
- Working to achieve business growth through the adroit use of tax mitigation strategies including helping to transfer wealth tax-efficiently between the generations
- Addressing significant personal matters such as adoptions and the children's education
- Planning vacations, parties, and other events
- Helping the family buy cars, planes, yachts, and islands
- Helping the family buy homes and making sure they and their contents are protected
- Finding and managing in-home cleaning, cooking, and support staff

- Acting as a barrier between family members and the outside world
- Managing family dynamics
- Finding support for family members in crisis
- Keeping private issues private and managing PR issues that arise

From a day-to-day perspective, this level of support brings great peace of mind to the family members. It enables the family to concentrate on the activities and areas they want to, knowing that these other matters are being well taken care of.

As families build wealth, they become more and more targeted by frivolous and unfounded lawsuits, people wanting to latch onto them, and scams. Having a family office in place provides the expertise that can put in place the appropriate barriers for protecting the family. Commonly, Single Family Offices help screen and filter people who are trying to gain access to the family or their funds to make sure family members are working with the best professionals, as opposed to all the people who are trying to take advantage of or exploit them.

The Single Family Office as a Profitable Operation

For some ultra-wealthy families, Single Family Offices are not just a justifiable expense, they are cash flow positive. The financial gains realized by the family more than make up for the cost of operating the family office. Those benefits come in many forms, including

- Superior investment performance
- All forms of tax savings
- Risk reduction
- Expense management

These financial benefits can add up to many millions of dollars for the family. However, with such high fixed costs involved in paying a full team of specialists and support staff, it can take a lot to achieve cash flow positivity. That's why the numbers on a Single Family Office only tend to make sense for families when they cross somewhere between $250 million and $500 million.

In short, ultra-wealthy families are using the family office model to both manage and achieve growth in their business and personal lives. The family sets goals and priorities, and their Single Family Office helps them achieve them. The benefits I mentioned are just some of the ways the wealthiest families have used Single Family Offices to optimize their lives. But all those benefits don't matter much for families who can't justify the cost. The Single Family Office system won't work for most successful families. And that's why I created the first Middle-Market Family Office™, which I called the DiNuzzo Middle-Market Family Office™: to change the model in such a way that it creates the same results for a family with significantly less wealth: families with a net worth of between $10 million and $100+ million, who generate more than $10 million in annual revenue, or who make $1 million per year, or who are rapidly approaching those numbers.

 ## Keys to Chapter

- Single Family Offices are expensive and thus are only established by the ultra-wealthy.
- There are significant benefits the ultra-wealthy have because of their Single Family Office.
- Ultra-wealthy families worth somewhere above $250 million of net worth have benefited by setting up Single Family Offices for decades.
- Single Family Offices can benefit every area of their clients' lives by managing family wealth, reducing risk, increasing and managing cash flow, improving family business operations, coordinating concierge medical care, coordinating security at home and abroad, addressing significant personal matters, or helping the family buy cars, planes, yachts, homes, islands, and more.
- Single Family Offices can function as profitable operations where benefits realized from centralization and economies of scale, superior invest-

ment performance, tax savings, risk reduction, and expense management exceed the operating costs of the Single Family Office.

- Because of the high operating costs, only the ultra-wealthy have enough income, net worth, and potential benefits to justify the expense of setting up a Single Family Office.

- Middle-market successful business owners and wealthy families with a net worth of between $10 million and $100+ million, who generate more than $10 million in annual revenue, or who make $1 million per year can achieve many of the same benefits of a Single Family Office through the first Middle-Market Family Office™, my DiNuzzo Middle-Market Family Office™.

Chapter 2

The Forgotten Demographic: Middle-Market Business Owners

You've followed your vision, worked hard, managed a ton of risk, and created a significant business. You've built substantial wealth inside and possibly outside your company. You've grown your family. You give to the community. You're worth $10 million or more. You make around $1 million or more in annual income, or your business generates annual revenues in excess of $10 million. Or you're fast approaching one or more of these benchmarks.

You're incredibly successful by anyone's definition.

To achieve a net worth of at least $10 million and/or generate $10 million or more in annual revenue for your business, you will need to have built a significant business, earned a high income, saved and invested diligently, or a combination of the three. No matter what combination you used to build your wealth, if you've achieved $10 million or more in net worth, you face many of the same issues as those who achieve $250 million or more, just on a smaller scale. For example

- You face multiple tax issues that could cost or make you hundreds of thousands of dollars or more.

- You have surplus wealth and want to make sure you make smart decisions as to how to invest this money.
- You have significant assets to secure and risks to manage.
- You are consistently faced with tough decisions to manage and maximize cash flow in both your business and personal life.
- You likely have a target on your back for scammers or other people wanting your time and money.
- You have family, financial, and philanthropic goals.

You likely face some if not all of those issues, just not at the scale of the ultra-wealthy. That means you can strongly benefit from the same level of expertise provided by Single Family Offices, just not at the scale (and expense) of a Single Family Office. So a Single Family Office won't work for you.

That challenge is what influenced me to create the DMMFO in the first place. I saw an entire group of hardworking people who had spent decades building a business and taking care of their families, but who were stuck in a giant void in the marketplace because the system designed to provide the level of support those people need was prohibitively expensive. They were almost stuck in "no man's land" with nobody serving them to the level they needed to be served. I have spent decades recreating the impact a Single Family Office can have on successful business owners and their companies without the fixed expenses of a Single Family Office to serve a very specific but forgotten demographic—middle-market businesses and their owners.

The Anatomy of the Forgotten Demographic

At this point, you might wonder whether you fall into the forgotten demographic that has the same needs as the ultra-wealthy but at a smaller scale. After working with hundreds of business owners, their companies, and their families, my advanced planning strategy team and I have identified three relevant factors you can use to answer that question: net worth, income, and entrepreneurship.

The reason these factors are relevant is because each of them tells me something about taxes, cash flow, risk, health, philanthropy, and potential family issues at the level where a specialist or cohesive team of specialists is needed to achieve significant benefit, find solutions to material problems, or both.

When it comes to net worth, if you've reached somewhere around $10 million, or more, you begin running into issues and opportunities where consulting an expert can make a big difference. For example

- You have meaningfully more financial and legal options available that can prove instrumental in helping you protect and grow your wealth.
- You start running into major estate planning issues that can cost you millions of dollars if not properly addressed.
- You can create significant additional cash flow to improve your day-to-day life in ways that matter to you.
- You're more likely to have a target on your back from people who want your time and money.

When it comes to income, if you've reached somewhere around $1 million, or more, you also begin running into issues and opportunities where consulting an expert can make a big difference. For example

- You have surplus wealth where you can take advantage of investment possibilities less affluent individuals are frozen out of.
- You get to the point where traditional investment models and retirement plans might not be enough to help you achieve your retirement goals.
- You are, many times, able to benefit from more sophisticated wealth planning resulting in a significant decrease in taxes.

When it comes to entrepreneurship, if you own a business, you also face unique issues and opportunities where consulting an expert can make a big difference. For example

- You have greater control over the taxes you pay and how you pay them.

- You make business decisions on a regular basis that can positively or negatively impact entity value in substantial ways, but you need to have the possibilities clearly delineated.
- You can take advantage of many tax-advantaged strategies and solutions to increase cash flow, improve profitability, create greater personal wealth, and grow your entity value.

If one of these three factors describes you, it's possible that you're being underserved if you're not receiving the level of service and capabilities that the ultra-wealthy are receiving from their Single Family Offices. If two of the three factors describe you, you're very likely being underserved. If all three of the factors describe you, you're highly likely being underserved if your experience is not consistent with the DMMFO way.

One Irrelevant Factor: Liquidity

Many successful middle-market business owners are surprised that liquidity isn't one of the factors describing the forgotten demographic. What if they've struggled for years with low or inconsistent cash flow? What if they own a business worth $25 million and earn $1 million per year but live paycheck to paycheck? How could they possibly take advantage of many of the benefits provided to ultra-wealthy families if they can barely pay their monthly bills?

The short answer is because the DMMFO creates liquidity. In fact, creating liquidity is one of the primary outcomes my clients experience with the DMMFO. My team and I have access to many tools that can quickly create liquidity.

In other words, if you are not very liquid but own a business, make $1 million or more per year, have a net worth of $10 million or more, and/ or generate $10 million or more in annual revenue in your business, the DMMFO can likely create the liquidity you need to increase and smooth out your cash flow.

Frankly, liquidity is rarely the problem with my DMMFO clients. It's almost always the symptom of the real problem: they are being underserved by professionals who can't help them because they simply don't know what they don't know.

What's Holding Many Successful Business Owners Back?

As I'll discuss in more detail in chapter 12, one of the greatest impacts DMMFO can have on your life is the ability to help you start to work on your business, not in your business. We help you optimize all the day-to-day activities in both your business and personal lives, including increasing and stabilizing cash flow and generating liquidity.

As we do, you will begin to experience a series of benefits that build off each other. For example, when we increase and stabilize cash flow and generate liquidity, you will begin to feel the freedom that comes from not having to put out fires all day just to sustain cash flow. That freedom, along with other optimization strategies, will allow you to focus on the highest and best use of your time—working on your business (and, for many clients, also strengthening their health, personal relationships, and more).

As Warren Buffett famously said, "I insist on a lot of time being spent, almost every day, to just sit and think. That is very uncommon in American business." Think about your day. When's the last time you were able to just sit and think for even a few minutes, let alone "a lot of time ... almost every day"? If it's been a while (or has never happened), you're likely being underserved in several areas—both inside your business and from your professionals.

But as you begin working *on* your business and not just *in* your business, you can start to significantly grow both the top line and the bottom line, increase entity value, and so on and so forth.

When I first start working with business owners, many are surprised by how much of an impact my team and I can make on their business and personal lives simply by orchestrating this one shift in their business. They've made it to the top of the business world. And they have sacrificed so much to get there—late nights, missed family celebrations, personal health challenges, and more. They worked that hard to build a better life for their spouses, children, and children's children. They have changed their family tree.

But they are so busy working in their business that they have no time to truly work on their business. They get so caught up in the day-to-day business that the big-picture, higher-impact items in their business and personal lives get pushed aside. That's where my team and I come in. My team of specialists and I can act as strategic consultants who help you optimize your business as well as your personal situation and get you out of having to put out fires all day and into the higher-impact role you deserve.

How Being Underserved Costs Entrepreneurs Millions

Entrepreneurs know that one of the best ways to build a high net worth is to start a business. That's because entrepreneurship gives them many, often leveraged benefits. They can earn a salary. They can get favorable tax treatment. They can get access to many retirement and investment options that are not available to employees. And they can build an entity with a value that represents a multiple of either revenue or profits.

That last benefit can help them build substantial wealth quickly. A company with $5 million in profits in an industry where businesses sell for five times profits would add $25 million to the business owner's net worth, alone. And if they added just $200,000 in profits, they would increase their net worth by another $1 million.

While that sounds great, it also magnifies the risk entrepreneurs take when they are being underserved. That's because it's not just the growth in their business that gets leveraged; the mistakes they make in business are leveraged too. If they make a $200,000 mistake, oversight, or missed opportunity, their net worth can easily drop by $1 million.

We all know mistakes happen in business. And we know that there is no way to eliminate all mistakes. But what if you could make fewer mistakes because you don't have to manage your entire family, philanthropy, and financial future on top of running your business? What if you could concentrate on your business when you were at your business because everything else was taken care of?

We also know that many entrepreneurs are forced to make decisions that benefit the entity in the short term to the detriment of the long term. This often occurs when a company struggles with inconsistent cash flow. That can cause a company to take on a project that is not ideal. And that often results in poor performance, unhappy customers, frustrated employees, and longer-term pain. Inconsistent cash flow can also cause a company to cut back on marketing for a period of time, draining their pipeline of future projects.

When you are being underserved, you need to figure out how to solve the cash flow problem. But you are being pulled in 100 different directions managing your business, family, philanthropy, and financial future. You barely have time to eat lunch. How can you be expected to solve sophisticated cash flow problems?

You need help in two ways. First, you need help freeing up more time for you to concentrate on your business. Second, you need help solving the underlying problem that forces you to make decisions that are not ideal for your long-term future.

Working with a well-coordinated team of professionals like the ones in the DMMFO helps in both of these ways. My team and I handle all the legwork involved in optimizing your business, family, philanthropy, and financial future based on our discovery process. That allows us to educate you on multiple viable options for you to choose from. Now, you're able to make an informed decision when choosing between the options. You don't have to worry about finding professionals who are not just trying to sell you something, leaving you to evaluate all the programs yourself. My team and I do that for you.

THE DINUZZO MIDDLE-MARKET FAMILY OFFICE WAY

Step **1** *Discovery Process Incorporating Human Element*

Step **2** *Research and Analysis to Develop Options and Present the Pros and Cons to the Owner*

Step **3** *Let Owners Do What They Do Best ... Make the Decision*

Many professionals are unsophisticated, lacking the experience or expertise to do this for you. And, frankly, many professionals are just trying to sell you their product. Others are going to bill you for every minute you talk with them, often charging you thousands of dollars just to answer a simple question for you.

In the end, my DMMFO helps you maximize opportunities, eliminate gaps and holes, and make fewer costly mistakes. Keep in mind that investment and spending mistakes outside of your business have a much lower impact on your net worth compared to investment and spending mistakes inside your business. That's because an investment loss of $100,000 doesn't get leveraged the same way that business mistakes get leveraged into reducing enterprise value. You just lose $100,000 with investment or spending mistakes.

Yet many people are much more sensitive to investment or spending mistakes than business mistakes.

The Warning Flag of the Single Solution "Professional"

Let's use $10 million just as a cutoff point for the sake of this discussion. You're worth $10 million and you own a successful business. There are things you can do that will mitigate taxes, increase your personal wealth, and make it more effective when you sell your company so you don't have to pay other taxes. You have many options.

That's important. If anyone suggests you have only one choice, it's likely they are just trying to sell you something. In these situations, they generally either sell only one tool or they sell multiple tools but want to push you into the one that makes them the most money. Even many "pretender" professionals know you have multiple options to mitigate taxes. They know there are things you can do to increase your personal wealth. And they know you can put some structures in place to save taxes for when you sell your company.

But "pretender" professionals don't know all the options you have. Frankly, not many well-meaning, experienced professionals know *all* of your options and, additionally, they are not a part of a sophisticated team. They don't work with successful business owners like you all day, every day like my team and I do. They don't have the benefit of having helped hundreds of accomplished business owners solve thousands of nuanced problems. They just don't know what they don't know.

That's why my DMMFO model is in such high demand. Having an extensive, well-coordinated team of specialists on your side led by someone who knows you, your goals and concerns, and your business is a game changer for most (if not just about all) successful business owners. As I get to know you well through my discovery process, I reach out to my team of internal and external specialists, ensure they understand all about you and your business, and identify what options make sense along with the pros and cons of each option. I usually go back and forth to narrow down the best solutions to the top ones to present to you. The specialists on my cohesive team, some of whom you will meet later in this book, are experts who spend all day, every day helping people just like you achieve goals and deal with concerns just like yours. Collectively, they know the entire scope of what's available to you plus all the questions to ask to determine what your best options might be. Importantly, they know the nuances involved that most professionals never acquire.

Even with that level of expertise, there is never a single perfect solution to help you achieve all your goals and mitigate all your concerns. Between my core team of experts and our extended network of some of the most specialized experts in the country, our process inevitably yields multiple high-impact solutions for our business owner clients.

I always start with discovering your business, family, and history, and what you want to accomplish. What can I do with the experts I have, which are a team of leading experts whose expertise covers the entire landscape? And if I don't have an expert for a particular nuance because an issue is so rare, I know how to find that expertise. I can quickly bring in what I call niche specialists to help with that one little nuance that comes up. For example, this frequently comes up with cross-border corporate and family issues. If you have a business with multiple locations and some of those locations are outside the U.S., I can access professionals who specialize in addressing some of the international and multijurisdictional tax implications to make transactions less costly.

Importantly, my bespoke DMMFO model operates completely aboveboard. Every transaction I carry out for my clients is a bright-line transaction. I have operated since 1989 on the principle of integrity. Every solution my team of specialists and I present to you is completely legal with a proven track record. I don't push the envelope. I simply leverage and coordinate a team of some of the world's foremost experts to help you achieve your goals and address your concerns.

My team and I are very systematic in how we approach our work for you. We're very methodical. We make sure all the i's are dotted and t's are crossed to not just make sure you achieve what you want to achieve in the best way possible but that you can also legally and business-wise justify everything we do for you if it's ever questioned. That's what this is all about. It's unfortunate that I feel the need to type this, but there are a lot of people who are *not* aboveboard, who push the envelope with untested theories, questionable strategies, or worse. These people get themselves, and especially their clients, in a lot of trouble.

I not only comprehensively and carefully vet the professionals I bring onto my cohesive team to ensure they are experts at what they do and personify integrity but I also vet the solutions they recommend and I develop with them to ensure you are getting the best outcomes and are protected.

I'm not talking about pushing the envelope with anything we do either. I'm talking about finding the perfectly legal and available solutions that a lot of professionals, and certainly a great many successful business owners, don't know about. And even within the professionals who are aware of these solutions, the vast majority of them don't know how they best fit within your specific goals and desires.

They don't know how to connect the options to your world and make sure they are the right solutions for your situation to get you the results you want.

Keys to Chapter

- Individuals who are worth $10 million or more, make around $1 million or more in annual income, or generate revenues in excess of $10 million in a business—or are fast approaching one or more of those benchmarks— have the same or substantially similar needs as the ultra-wealthy in terms of complexity.

- This group of people needs the same level of expertise as the ultra-wealthy. They just don't have the same volume of issues. They don't need and can't justify the expense of having a full-time staff of the best-of-the-best experts serving them.

- This group of people has fallen through the cracks of the private wealth world. They cannot justify the expense of setting up a Single Family Office but have needs that require more expertise than the typical professional can provide.

- Because of that, this group of entrepreneurs and families has become the forgotten demographic and has been underserved in a way that has cost them millions of dollars.

- Many professionals in the wealth management world know that this demographic needs higher-level solutions, and so they market themselves as sophisticated professionals. In reality, the vast majority of them are "pretenders." Many of them steer clients to a single solution that makes the professional the most money instead of providing options and helping the client make an informed decision about the best solution for them. Beware of anyone in the investment world that attempts to steer you toward a single solution.

Chapter 3

The Problems with Traditional Single Family Offices and Other Solutions for the Forgotten Demographic of Middle-Market Business Owners

To demonstrate the problems with traditional Single Family Offices and other solutions that are currently underserving the forgotten demographic, let's focus for a minute on how you would recommend operating a business.

If you were hiring a new CFO, what type of background would you want in your new hire? If you're like most business owners, you would obviously prefer someone with a financial background, right? What about experience? Would you prefer someone just starting out, with a few years of experience, or someone with decades of experience? What about industry specialty? Wouldn't it be helpful to have someone who understands your industry? Of course it would. If your business could afford your ideal hire, they would likely be a highly specialized financial professional with decades of experience working in your industry.

What about a chief operating officer? If you could afford your ideal hire, they would also likely be a specialized professional with decades of experience in your industry too.

What about a chief legal officer? Would you prefer someone straight out of law school or someone with the experience and expertise to handle your most pressing legal issues?

What about a chief marketing officer?

Or a chief technology officer?

Or an executive assistant?

What qualities and experience level would you want from them?

And who would make sure all of these people in your business are working as a single, well-coordinated unit, all working together and heading in the same direction?

The ideal business would be led by an experienced chief executive officer who leads a team of experienced specialists who all work seamlessly together toward a common goal.

And that's how big multinational conglomerates operate, constantly competing for the best-of-the-best talent in every position in the company. They work consistently to outbid and out recruit each other for the top talent in the world.

What does this have to do with traditional Single Family Offices and other solutions?

That's *exactly* how a Single Family Office operates.

A Single Family Office is made up of the best-of-the-best specialists all working toward optimizing their "business": the lives of the ultra-wealthy family they have been hired to serve. These specialists, some of whom work full-time in the Single Family Office and others who work part-time, are charged with bringing other experts to the table on an as-needed basis when the in-house expertise is lacking. These specialists are senior executives adept not only at their areas of expertise but also at finding external experts the family needs and coordinating these specialists. It's led by a chief executive officer responsible for finding, hiring, and leading experienced internal and external specialists to make sure the family office owner's family, financial, and philanthropic worlds are fully optimized.

Unfortunately, hiring the right level of senior talent and experience costs a lot of money. A senior executive of a Single Family Office could easily cost hundreds of thousands of dollars per year or more. At some Single Family Offices, the senior executives earn millions of dollars annually as well as a percentage of the investment returns. Even a small Single Family Office employs a handful of people on a full-time basis. Imagine needing a dozen high-quality professionals, each of them commanding a high salary and a potential percentage of returns based on their level of experience.

Very, very few middle-market business owners can justify the cost required to operate a full-time Single Family Office to run their lives, including coordinating outside experts. It would not provide a sufficient return on investment to commit to the expense for even a small family office staff.

So what does the middle-market business owner or affluent family do? Alternatives are limited.

Here's what most middle-market business owners have traditionally done.

Existing Options for Middle-Market Business Owners

As I discuss the traditional options, let's start with the premise that successful middle-market business owners have similar needs to the ultra-wealthy. They have complex business and family dynamics. Cookie-cutter solutions won't work well for them, and all too commonly this one-size-fits-all approach can be detrimental. They need a well-coordinated team of experts who know how to spot gaps and identify opportunities for them so they can optimize their lives. And they need those experts to work within a compensation model that makes sense for everyone involved. As you'll see, however, existing options sacrifice expertise, expense, or both.

One option for middle-market business owners involves hiring less experienced or less capable professionals and having one of them act as a team leader. As we have discussed so far, however, less experienced or less specialized professionals don't know what they don't know. And in the world of successful middle-market business owners, that often results in you paying hundreds of thousands of dollars in unnecessary taxes, leaving assets unreasonably exposed to risk, poorly investing to match your objectives, and losing out on countless opportunities to otherwise optimize your life. Hiring a less experienced or less capable professional would defeat the purpose of hiring a professional to be your team leader.

Another option for middle-market business owners involves taking command and acting as their own personal CEO. In this scenario, the CEO (you) would hire and manage a number of specialists. This is what many middle-market business owners currently try to do when they realize how much they can benefit from having a true, well-coordinated team of specialists serving them.

In practice, however, acting as your own CEO to manage a number of leading experts can be equally as costly and as ineffective as hiring less experienced or less capable professionals and having one of them act as a team leader.

First, would you hire a CEO who has a full-time job running another company to run a $10 million+ company? Of course you wouldn't. Yet that's essentially what you are doing when you try to manage all the professionals yourself.

Second, to be able to build the knowledge and spend the time needed to effectively lead a team of professionals, you would probably need to turn your attention away from your primary business. If you pulled away enough time and attention from your business to lead a team of specialists, your primary business could suffer.

Third, you know what you know. You can quickly spot issues and lead people in your business. You can't reasonably expect yourself to be able to know and hire the ideal specialists for each issue that will come up. Even if you do, you probably don't know what questions to ask or what each professional needs to know to serve you exceptionally well. For instance, if you're thinking of selling a part of your company, are you aware of all the strategies you can use to either defer, mitigate, or eliminate taxes on the sale?

Fourth, hiring the best-of-the-best professionals with the right experience and specialization through traditional engagements is *still* expensive. Professionals at these levels may require a large retainer and likely charge hundreds of dollars an hour when you hire them traditionally. Many lawyers at this level will charge over $1,000 an hour. And they charge for every minute they think about you (in 6- or 15-minute blocks of time). If you send them an email on a Monday evening, they charge you to read it. If they reply the next morning, they charge you for their time spent responding. When they get into the work, they charge for every second they analyze options for you, even if you end up not moving forward with *any* of them. You could spend tens of thousands of dollars just to learn that your best option is to do nothing.

Fifth, even if you do find the right professionals to serve you, experts at this level generally don't work well together without a coordinating mechanism, or quarterback, such as another knowledgeable professional who understands all the possibilities and keeps the experts on track. This doesn't usually happen outside of the family office setting. An accountant wants to work with other professionals in their firm. They want to work with lawyers with whom they have existing relationships. They often want to make certain you buy what they provide. Getting professionals to communicate and consistently work well together with people outside of their organizations is next to impossible—or at least extremely rare—when putting the team together and leading it yourself.

These are just some of the reasons that existing options for middle-market business owners can be exasperating.

In the end, you don't get the level of service or the solutions you truly can benefit from unless you spend more than you can justify. If you try to manage things yourself, you still may end up spending more than you can afford, and your results rarely justify the effort.

How to Solve the Problem

When I started my DiNuzzo Middle-Market Family Office™, I made it my mission to solve this problem. My goal was to create the first expert-led, well-coordinated team of best-of-the-best specialists whose sole purpose was to optimize the financial and personal lives of middle-market business owners.

In order to achieve that objective, three things needed to be true.

- First, the experts needed to be leading specialists in their fields with commensurate track records and be recognized by their peers as such. The level of service and expertise needed to be the exact same as that enjoyed by the ultra-wealthy.

- Second, that team needed to work seamlessly together and work well with existing professionals the client has in place. If a risk management specialist was implementing a solution, the attorney needed to understand what to prepare, the tax specialist had to know what to do, and every other team member who needed to be involved was involved working for the betterment of the business owner.

- Third, the model could only charge based on the value received by the client for the solutions they actually use. Regularly, we will conduct a lot of analytic work to ascertain which possible solutions actually are viable. Our clients do not pay for these analyses; they only pay for results.

These three things would solve all the problems with the traditional methods: service, coordination, and cost.

In the next chapter, I'll show you how I solved that problem to create the first family office designed exclusively for middle-market business owners and affluent families, my DMMFO.

Keys to Chapter

- A Single Family Office is made up of the best-of-the-best specialists all working toward optimizing their "business": the lives of the ultra-wealthy family they have been hired to serve.

- Very, very few middle-market business owners can justify the cost required to operate a full-time Single Family Office to run their lives, including coordinating outside experts.

- Successful middle-market business owners have similar needs to the ultra-wealthy. They deserve a well-coordinated team of experts who know how to spot gaps and identify opportunities for them so they can optimize their lives. And they require those experts to work within a compensation model that makes sense for everyone involved.

- Existing options include Single Family Offices and the client trying to oversee a team of professionals. These options suffer from three big problems: (1) limited or inconsistent levels of service, (2) poor coordination among professionals, and (3) high costs.

- In order to solve those three problems, a solution needs three qualities. First, the experts need to be leading specialists in their fields and be recognized by their peers as such. Second, that team needs to work seamlessly together and work well with existing professionals the client has in place. Third, the model must only charge based on the value received by the client for the solutions they actually use.

PART 2:

———

The Big Breakthrough for Privately Held Business Owners: The DiNuzzo Middle-Market Family Office™

———

Chapter 4

The Private Wealth Hierarchy

To achieve your optimal business, financial, family, and philan-
thropic world and enjoy an amazing life of significance, you need to
work with the right professionals and the ones who are best for you.

With all your daily challenges, along with everything else going on in the world economically, politically, and socially, you owe it to your loved ones and yourself to stop, reflect, and ask yourself:

"Am I well-positioned with my financial affairs to achieve everything that
is important to me?"

My team and I are obsessed with helping every one of our clients live their best life. We are focused on this so they can (1) take care of themselves and the people they love, (2) fully support the causes they care about, and (3) make a difference in this world.

But one of the primary hurdles standing in the way of so many successful individuals, couples, and families achieving their best life is that they don't understand how the wealth management and family office worlds are structured. They don't know that there exists a hierarchy of service and capabilities in the world of private wealth.

Even worse, many business owner clients come to me believing they are receiving the best available care when they are really receiving much less care than they need and deserve. They're being served by people on the bottom of the Private Wealth Hierarchy—where the offerings are limited—when they really need and deserve to be served by people operating at the top of the hierarchy who are able to holistically and synergistically address their diverse needs, wants, and concerns.

When that happens, the only people who lose are the business owner clients. The professionals serving them from the bottom of the hierarchy may in fact be good at what they do, but it's very limited and often fails to produce optimal results. Commonly, the products and services they pitch are rarely the best fit for the client—they're just what the professionals sell.

I have seen this many times as my team and I conduct our discovery process or stress test someone's investment or wealth plans. It's not uncommon for us to identify hundreds of thousands of dollars (or more) in taxes that didn't need to be paid, excess insurance premiums paid, unnecessary risk exposure, misalignment of investments and goals, or lost opportunities that the professionals who had been serving our clients had missed. But without understanding the Private Wealth Hierarchy, many clients won't even know what questions to ask to determine whether they are being underserved.

Of course, not all existing professionals serving our clients fall into this category. Many of them are excellent service providers but are focused on only one specialty. In these cases, I work closely with those existing professionals and bring in only the professionals needed to fill any gaps in experience or expertise required to help my client achieve their goals.

Questions to Ask Yourself to Assess Whether You're Being Underserved

There exists a hierarchy of professionals in the financial industry as it applies to successful middle-market business owners and affluent families with less than $250 million in net worth. I call this grading the Private Wealth Hierarchy.

The bottom of the hierarchy offers the most limited level of capabilities and services. At the top is my DiNuzzo Middle-Market Family Office™, or DMMFO, structure, which provides the same level of care and service that the Single Family Offices provide to the world's richest people. I'll describe each of the four levels of skill and service in more detail below.

As I share the hierarchy with you, take a moment to look at the level of service you're receiving from the professionals who are advising you. What level of care are you getting? Where on the hierarchy is your level of service? Is it at the bottom? In the middle? Are you satisfied with the range of expertise and capabilities you're receiving, or do you want more? If you want more, then you need to move up the hierarchy.

I also want you to think about where you are from a business, financial, family, and philanthropic perspective. Are you where you want to be? Will your business operate smoothly without you having to do everything yourself? Are you minimizing your taxable income? Are you effectively mitigating taxes on your investment portfolio? If the answer to any of those questions is no, you deserve better.

The Private Wealth Hierarchy for Successful Middle-Market Business Owners

In the wealth management world, there are generally four levels of service, starting with the "Investment Advisor" at the bottom of the hierarchy. Slightly above the Investment Advisor is the "Financial Advisor." Above the Financial Advisor is the "Wealth Manager." And at the very top of the pyramid is my "DiNuzzo Middle-Market Family Office™."

Until my DMMFO, only the ultra-wealthy could receive the family office level of service. There were essentially only three levels of service available to 99 percent of business owners. Below you will find a brief description of each level in the hierarchy.

While any one of these levels might be right for you, the great majority of middle-market business owners prefer the top of the hierarchy. As you read through the four options and continue through the rest of my book, ask yourself which level of care, service, and protection you'd prefer.

Warning: Many Professionals Market Themselves as Higher-Level Service Providers Than They Truly Are

Before you move forward, let me warn you that many professionals hold themselves out as higher-level service providers than they truly are. They use buzzwords in their firm names and marketing materials that suggest they provide higher levels of care than they actually provide.

This problem is pervasive. In my experience, the vast majority of wealth management professionals do this. For instance, many Investment Advisors—"Level 1" professionals in the hierarchy—call themselves "multi-family offices," suggesting they provide a similar level of coordination, expertise, specialization, and service as my DMMFO. They misrepresent themselves because they know that the term "family office" carries weight in the private wealth world. So they cobble together a few helpful referral relationships with other professionals and market themselves as "multi-family offices" in order to win over potential clients. Unfortunately, their new clients quickly find out that they were "misinformed" (to put it kindly). They become bombarded with high fees. They discover their "team" is neither expert nor value-driven, charging the client for every phone call and supposed "research." They are often even steered toward products or services based on what the professionals make the most money providing, even if there's a better fit but that product or service doesn't make money for the professionals.

To avoid this result, you need to cut through the marketing façade and focus instead on what your relationship with them will look like when you hire them. To do so, evaluate these factors about the professionals who would be serving you if you move forward: (1) the level of experience and specialization of the professionals serving you, (2) how many services you would receive, (3) how coordinated the team of professionals would be, (4) how many goals your professionals would help you achieve, and (5) how they would charge for their products or services.

"Investment Advisors": A Single Service with a Single Goal

At the bottom of the Private Wealth Hierarchy is the "Investment Advisor." The Investment Advisor operates using a model with which most business owners and wealthy families are familiar. Investment Advisors have been around for decades and make themselves available to just about anyone with capital to invest.

The Investment Advisor focuses solely on investments. At this level, you will receive a single level of service and you have a single goal: to grow the value of the assets you invest with the advisor. Your relationship is totally focused on running money, managing money, investing your assets. That's it. Even with a talented Investment Advisor, your relationship will only produce a myopic level of confidence because it's just a single-purpose service. Your advisor is only managing assets and not tying this service into anything else. They don't help you with estate planning or other family goals. They don't help improve cash flow in your business. They don't help you access better healthcare. They only manage assets you entrust to them.

Investment Advisors, for example, can be helpful for the mass affluent or people who just need help choosing investments in their retirement accounts. If *all* you want is someone to invest your money, and you're not interested in ways to not only achieve solid investment returns but also maximize other aspects of your and your family's life, then you can stop at this level. Most middle-market business owners tend to have complex needs, wants, and preferences, and they need more expertise from their professionals.

"Financial Advisors": Limited Service with Moderate Goals

The next level on the Private Wealth Hierarchy is that of a "Financial Advisor." At the Financial Advisor level, there is a limited level of service and capabilities, which is up from the single level service you receive when working with an Investment Advisor.

Because Financial Advisors do slightly more than the Investment Advisor, they can generally help you achieve more, but still only modest goals. However, for the most part, the additional levels of service are mostly limited to some basic financial planning. They don't help you with more intricate estate planning or other nonfinancial family goals. They don't help improve cash flow in your business or help to maximize the value. They also don't help you access better healthcare. At this level, they act in a facilitator capacity—at best.

Financial Advisors are essentially Investment Advisors who also do some financial planning for you. Financial Advisors can certainly be helpful for people who are beginning to earn six figures, want to set up a basic strategy to save for college or retirement, or want help with very basic wealth planning and investing for long-term goals, such as homeownership.

"Wealth Managers": Extensive Service with Respect to the Big Five Goals

As people begin to accumulate wealth and have more needs and objectives, they tend to ascend to the third level of the Private Wealth Hierarchy by working with a "Wealth Manager."

True Wealth Managers typically serve clients with between $1 million and $10 million of investment assets. At the wealth management level, you receive a broad level of services, based on your more extensive goals and concerns with the focus on achieving what I refer to as the Big Five Goals, which include the following:

- Helping you make smart decisions about your money, including investing
- Mitigating taxes and engaging in proactive tax management
- Taking care of your heirs
- Enhancing charitable giving and charitable planning
- Protecting your assets from being unjustly taken through litigation and divorce

This experience gives clients what I call a quiet and extensive confidence. True Wealth Managers who work at this level are generally more experienced and sophisticated than most Investment Advisors and Financial Advisors. Between their experience, level of service, and attention to the Big Five Goals, their clients achieve what I describe as a quiet and extensive level of confidence in their financial future.

In addition to their individual experience, Wealth Managers have built an impressive professional network of other experts, such as tax attorneys, estate planning attorneys, private client attorneys, accountants, risk management specialists, and others. This network helps Wealth Managers deliver world-class experiences to clients on their Big Five Goals.

Unfortunately, the term "wealth management" has become a buzzword in the wealth advisory world. It's become a marketing term. And that's caused many Investment Advisors or Financial Advisors to market themselves as Wealth Managers when they do not provide true wealth management services. In fact, the vast majority of professionals marketing themselves as Wealth Managers do not offer true wealth management services. They will include "wealth management" in their name or promotional materials for marketing misdirection, but the level of service they provide is that of a Financial Advisor, at best. That has caused a lot of successful business owners to get underserved while believing they were receiving the highest level of care available to them.

DiNuzzo Middle-Market Family Office™: Full Service for all Business, Financial, Family, and Philanthropic Goals

At the very top of the hierarchy, you will find the best-of-the-best professionals. Less than 1 percent of professionals ever ascend to the level where they have the skills and cohesive team of specialists to provide world-class care to clients no matter what their business, financial, family, or philanthropic goals are. As mentioned earlier, you needed a minimum net worth of about $250 million for the family office model to work for you and your family. It was just too expensive to operate if you were worth less than that.

However, as I worked with more successful business owners who fell into the forgotten demographic, I realized that the problem with accessibility to family offices was solvable. If highly specialized professionals utilized technology and changed their compensation structure to a value-only model, I could provide a best-of-the-best service to people who had much less wealth than the ultra-wealthy: the forgotten demographic making $1 million per year, generating revenue of $10 million in their business, and/or having a net worth of $10 million or more (or fast approaching those milestones).

Professionals at this level must also have an extensive network of other professionals who are the best-of-the-best specialists in their field at their disposal. Individual professionals or single-firm structures cannot deliver the level of experience or specialization necessary to cover all subject matter needed to provide the right level of services to successful middle-market business owners.

The Private Wealth Advisor and all professionals who work on the advisor's team need to be comfortable bringing in other leading professionals to serve the best interests of the client. They also need to be able to seamlessly coordinate these experts to leverage the skills and expertise of each member of the team and make sure they serve their client well.

Additionally, the professionals on the team need to be comfortable working with the Private Wealth Advisor and other experts. They need to be able to recommend and present possible solutions for even the most sophisticated problems or goals in such a way that helps clients make informed choices from among several options. They then need to be able to implement the solution the client chooses.

In the end, the Private Wealth Advisor and team need to be willing and able to pull together into one cohesive, well-coordinated team with a singular goal of helping the business owner clients achieve their goals and address their concerns.

These factors, and others, make the family office extremely difficult to pull off for even the most experienced Wealth Advisors. That's why less than 1 percent of professionals ever ascend to this level. Even those who have the skills needed to do their part struggle to pull together the network of best-of-the-best specialists. And those who pull together the best-of-the-best specialists often fail to find specialists who can work well together. Or they can't crack the code of pulling it all together in a way that puts the clients' needs above their own income goals.

Frankly, the vast majority of professionals don't work well together. When a lawyer or accountant rises to the top of their profession after decades of experience, they often get set in their ways and, justifiably, confident in their methods. They're also extremely busy, and many of them work in larger firms that like to keep work in-house with their in-house employees. All that leads to them not working well with others, especially outside of their firm. In order for the family office model to work, however, each specialist needs to work well with others and be the best-of-the-best in their field. That's why I have remained completely independent. I sit on the same side of the table as my clients and look out for their best interests. I ensure that I have no conflicts of interest so my clients can rest assured that the solutions I present to them are not influenced by anything other than what will best help them achieve their goals.

But when it all comes together, family office services are truly life changing for clients across every aspect of their business, financial, family, and philanthropic lives. Over the rest of this book, I'll show you exactly what that level of service looks like. I'll also show you how I've been able to crack the code to quarterback and orchestrate the same level of service and expertise once reserved only for the ultra-wealthy but now available to middle-market business owners too.

And I'll show you how my DiNuzzo Middle-Market Family Office™ (DMMFO) can help you maximize your goals and your lifestyle, helping you achieve comprehensive results in all areas of your business, family, personal, and philanthropic life—well beyond the Big Five Goals.

The Big Problem with the Bottom Three Options: Where Most Investment Advisors, Financial Advisors, and Wealth Managers Go Wrong

Nothing will bias a man's perspective more than something directly related to the paycheck he's receiving.—**Unknown**

In my experience, most Investment Advisors, Financial Advisors, and Wealth Managers don't intend to harm their clients. Sure, a lot of them push their clients to buy the products they sell, irrespective of fit. However, even those professionals don't believe that their products are harming their clients. They convince themselves that their products make their clients' lives better. The irreversible/fatal flaw is that they are looking at everything in a vacuum.

But that's the problem. Most Investment Advisors, Financial Advisors, and Wealth Managers aim too low by not looking objectively or at the big picture; they come into their relationships believing "better" is good enough for their clients. Thus, if they can improve their clients' lives even slightly, in their mind, they've done their job.

Only a small percentage of Wealth Managers—less than 1 percent in my experience—know that "better" is *not* good enough and therefore deliver the best-of-the-best value for their clients. For successful business owners and wealthy families, the best-of-the-best is within reach—but only *if* they can work with the right professionals who are truly client-focused and structure the relationship in a value-driven manner.

That level of service happens only *at the top* of the Private Wealth Hierarchy in a structure once only reserved for the ultra-wealthy: the family office and, for middle-market business owners, my DMMFO.

What Makes My DiNuzzo Middle-Market Family Office™ a Breakthrough to Solve This Problem (and Others)

When other professionals learn about my DMMFO model, they are often surprised by my ability to provide a true Single Family Office experience and value within a model that works for The Forgotten Demographic.

It took years of innovation and optimization for my DMMFO to achieve a true Single Family Office level of service. But, once I got there, the combination of the following six important factors finally allowed my DMMFO clients to experience the level of expertise and service they needed and deserved:

1. **Virtual.** My specialists and I can do everything we need to do completely virtually. Today, more people and professionals are capable of and comfortable working virtually than ever before. (The COVID-19 pandemic has opened up even more professionals' minds to the idea of helping people virtually.)

2. **Technology.** Technological advances have provided me with sophisticated industry tools and communication technology to connect with people all around the world in a matter of seconds.

3. **A Non-Sales, Truly Consultative Approach.** Unlike the typical professional, I don't go into any conversation looking to sell anything. I look to identify my clients' goals and help find the solutions to achieve them. I educate my clients about their options, which often don't result in my earning a penny. Then, my clients decide which option works best for them, if any.

4. **Expert Private Wealth Advisor P. J. DiNuzzo.** My DMMFO clients can rest assured that the options I present to them have been personally vetted by me, that any experts who support them are among the best-of-the-best in the world for what my clients need, and that they will have all the information necessary to make informed decisions.

5. **Natural Market Factors.** Natural market factors have created more opportunities for successful middle-market business owners across multiple areas of focus. For example, just like cell phones were once only available to the ultra-wealthy, natural market factors have caused many solutions that were once only available to the ultra-wealthy to become available to successful middle-market business owners.

6. **Specialists Willing to Expand Their Footprint.** Years ago, specialists operating at the Single Family Office level had no need or desire to expand their footprint. Over time, competition, hyper-specialization, and the ease with which they can work virtually made them more willing to expand into new markets.

As my wealth management clients' needs expanded, I committed to expanding alongside them, and that's how the big breakthrough took place. I understood how Single Family Offices operated. I knew what level of services and expertise they provided to their ultra-wealthy clients. And I also knew that my clients' needs were no different: they required the same level of sophistication and expertise from their professionals to achieve their goals.

With me acting as a "conductor" to coordinate the right mix of specialists to serve each client's unique goals and desires, my DMMFO utilizes a *cohesive* team-within-a-team-within-a-team approach to create *integrated* solutions for my clients. My three teams that combine to serve each of my DMMFO clients include the following.

Inner Circle Team
(Four Foundational Specialists and Their Boutique Teams)

- Center of Influence and Core Topic Specialists Team
  - Legal: Trusts and Estates, Asset Protection, Succession, and Exit Planning
  - Tax: Tax Planning, Tax Preparation, and Tax Strategy
  - Risk: Risk Planning, Risk Strategy, Transfer, and Coordination, Personal Lines, and Property & Casualty
  - Wealth Planning and Wealth Management

Middle Circle Team
(20+ Team Members)

- Wealth Management
- Tax
- Risk
- Insurance
- Cash-Flow
- Investment
- Lifestyle

Outer Circle Team
(30+ Experts and Their Teams)

- DiNuzzo Middle-Market Family Office™ Advanced Planning Strategy Team of Experts, who typically have Single Family Office experience, along with the commensurate *bona fides* and expertise to address the most complex, nuanced, and specialized domestic, inbound, cross-border, and international needs.

Together, there's no issue that I haven't been able to help my clients navigate using my team-within-a-team-within-a-team approach.

Myth: Doing Better Is Good Enough

At best, the vast majority of professionals in the wealth management space only help you become incrementally better in one, or maybe two, of the Big Five Goals. An Investment Advisor may help you manage assets better. A Financial Advisor may help you plan how to achieve one or two longer-term goals. A Wealth Manager may help you make extensive progress toward achieving your Big Five Goals.

That's as good as it got for people worth less than $250 million for decades. There was simply no way to achieve optimal results. Professionals lacked the sophistication, experience, or network to help you beyond the Big Five Goals. Even those who had the sophistication, experience, or network either couldn't or didn't play well with other professionals in their network, preferring to keep as much work as possible "in-house," even if another expert was truly the best-of-the-best in their field. And, even if they worked well with others, the vast majority of those professionals couldn't or didn't want to structure the relationship in a way that worked best for you.

As a result, the forgotten demographic has been told they were receiving the best available service when, in fact, they have been systemically underserved for decades.

Truth: The Best-of-the-Best Is within Your Reach

I know the best-of-the-best is within your reach because I built my DMMFO to provide just that. I've been doing it for years, decades even. But every piece of the puzzle is needed for it to work. You'll need

- an experienced Private Wealth Advisor as the point person for your care;
- a process for discovering even the most nuanced gaps and opportunities and providing you with viable options and information to allow you to make informed decisions;
- a well-coordinated team of best-of-the-best specialists, who are not all under one roof but play seamlessly together to fill in gaps of experience and expertise left open by existing professionals currently serving you—and even work very well with any existing professionals who are serving you well;
- a vast extended network of best-of-the-best specialists who are available at a moment's notice to help with issues that come up only occasionally; and
- a compensation model that puts client value above all else, including their own financial benefit.

If your professionals don't check all those boxes, one of two things is generally happening. First, they are serving you well but only in one or two narrow areas of specialty. In these cases, my team and I can fill in those gaps of experience or expertise. Second, they are aiming too low—aiming for "better," not the best-of-the-best for you and your family. And if they aim too low, at best, you will get what you aim for. You're the one likely taking unnecessary risk. You're the one likely paying too many taxes. You're the one likely stuck working in your business instead of on your business. You're the one whose family likely needs to worry about what will happen if you pass away. Very likely, your business is at risk. Not theirs. Theirs is fine—you're buying all their products and services. But you deserve "better than better." You deserve the best-of-the-best. And you only get the best-of-the-best with the solution I put together for my DMMFO. That's how you receive the comprehensive level of service you deserve.

In the next chapter, I'll show you exactly how my DMMFO helps you get that value.

 Keys to Chapter

- There exists a hierarchy in the private wealth industry.
- At the bottom of the Private Wealth Hierarchy is the Investment Advisor. Investment Advisors can be helpful for middle-income earners or people who just need help choosing investments in their retirement accounts.
- The next level on the Private Wealth Hierarchy is that of a Financial Advisor. Financial Advisors are essentially Investment Advisors who also do very limited financial planning for you, and many times begrudgingly.
- As people begin to accumulate wealth and have more needs and objectives, they tend to ascend to the third level of the Private Wealth Hierarchy by working with a Wealth Manager. The Wealth Manager's network of other experts, such as tax attorneys, estate planning attorneys, private client attorneys, accountants, risk management specialists helps them deliver world-class experiences to clients on their Big Five Goals: investing and

other money decisions, tax mitigation and management, taking care of your heirs, charitable giving and planning, and asset protection.

- At the very top of the hierarchy, you will find the best-of-the-best professionals. Less than 1 percent of professionals ever ascend to the level where they have the skills and cohesive team of specialists to provide world-class care to clients no matter what their business, financial, family, or philanthropic goals are.

- Many professionals hold themselves out as higher-level service providers than they truly are. They use buzzwords in their firm names and marketing materials that suggest they provide higher levels of care than they actually provide.

Chapter 5

How the DiNuzzo Middle-Market Family Office™ Gives Middle-Market Business Owners the Best of Both Worlds

When I engage in my discovery process and learn new clients' interests, goals, concerns, and current levels of service, I almost always find that most middle-market business owners are being underserved. I do so by going into my discovery process with what I call, "professional ignorance" (uber-objectivity), which means that I don't assume anything about you or your goals, despite having served successful middle-market business owners since 1989. Instead, I go into each relationship looking to learn as much as I can about you, your present circumstances, and your goals for the future.

When I complete my initial discovery process, I frequently learn that my near client has been dealing primarily with a bunch of professionals who are each trying to sell their services or products to them. Some of them have one or two trusted advisors. But aside from those advisors, almost every meeting with these people ends up being a sales pitch. Nobody takes any significant time considering how their product or service would impact the bigger picture of their client's life, such as what the

55

client actually wants for their family or the impact of their product or service on the business. Instead, these "professionals" essentially tell the client what the client *should* want, which just so happens to be what the professional sells.

At my DiNuzzo Middle-Market Family Office™, we know there's a better way. We specialize in serving successful middle-market owners, so we know a lot about what they want in general. For example, most family business owners want to minimize their taxes. But we also know that minimizing taxes and other common desires are generic goals that mean something different to different families. And we know that nobody goes through life with a single goal. In this context, nobody *just* wants to minimize taxes. They want to do other things, too, such as growing the business, enjoying their life in the present, taking care of their families and others, and so forth. Thus, the solutions for "minimizing taxes" will not be the same for every client.

For example, there are certain types of sophisticated retirement plans that will enable business owners to really lower their income taxes dramatically. But, like everything in the private wealth world, there are trade-offs. In this example, the retirement plan does lower their income taxes dramatically because it allows business owners to significantly defer paying taxes on a lot of money. However, the family no longer has immediate access to the money because they put it in the plan. So this type of plan might not be the best fit for families who want to reinvest the money back in their business. Other sophisticated tax minimization strategies will likely be a better choice for a family like this. Contrast that with a family that doesn't need access to the money and is more concerned with minimizing taxes and protecting large amounts of money. A strategy like this would make more sense for them.

Just like not all businesses are the same, not all solutions for the business owner's goals will be the same. Your world and your desires are way more nuanced and sophisticated than that. True family office professionals work to understand all of your most important goals so they can help you choose the best solution in your case. It's not my job to tell you which way is the best. It's my job to show you the options we believe can best help you achieve your goals and then you decide which direction you want to go.

From working with thousands of business owners, we've learned that most professionals never develop a clue which strategy is truly best for their clients because they don't invest the time in talking to them to really understand all the issues involved. They don't understand family dynamics, what roles the family members are best suited to fill, what roles the family needs help with, and any number of other considerations. They often have blinders on and consequently recommend cookie-cutter solutions that might work on the surface but don't fully account for the family's bigger goals and needs.

The better way is to—when possible—present multiple options to the family, along with the pros and cons of each, all framed within the context of that family's needs and goals. That's important because there's rarely only one potential solution to solving a problem or achieving a goal. There are usually multiple possible solutions. Unfortunately, too many advisors see a surface-level issue and move right to the sales pitch. If they sell something like a nonqualified deferred compensation plan, which many companies use to incentivize executives, they'll steer the conversation toward the value of attracting and incentivizing a nonfamily member to work in their business, and then start to pitch their "solution" to your problem. Even if attracting nonfamily members is one goal of yours, there are many ways to do this, and whatever they sell is not the right plan for every family.

That's what this is all about. It's taking time for each of these situations, each of these successful middle-market family business owners, each of these companies, and really drilling down to what they want. Then it's about coordination among professionals to offer multiple potential solutions, along with the pros and cons of each, in such a way that allows the client to make an informed decision about which option they want for their family.

This approach is not unique to saving taxes, maximizing retirement plans, or incentivizing executives. You can find salespeople disguised as "professionals" in every discipline. Take succession planning, for example. The minute most professionals hear those buzzwords, they jump in with their succession planning "solution." They explain how it works and all the benefits their plan has to offer. Again, none of what they say may be false, but that doesn't mean their "solution" is the right fit for every family. You have multiple options for succession planning. Some will be a good fit. Some will be a poor fit. And some could even destroy your business and tear your family apart.

For example, what if nobody wants to inherit the business? Forcing a business onto a family member who doesn't want it could destroy their life. What if someone wants to inherit the business, but they live in another state and have no desire to move? You might need to involve more nonfamily leadership on-site and set up a structure that allows the business to thrive without the owner being in-state. What if you have six children, one who wants to inherit the business but isn't qualified to work in it, two who are interested in inheriting it and want to work in the business, and three who have no interest in inheriting or working in the business? No cookie-cutter "solution" will solve all those challenges. Unfortunately, most advisors would pitch the same or similar "solutions" in each scenario.

The Secret Sauce: The Six Factors That Allow for Seamless Coordination among the Best-of-the-Best Professionals

As I mentioned in chapter 4, the combination of six factors has helped me provide my DMMFO clients with the level of expertise and service they need and deserve:

1. Virtual
2. Technology
3. A Non-Sales, Truly Consultative Approach
4. Expert Private Wealth Advisor P. J. DiNuzzo
5. Natural Market Factors
6. Specialists Willing to Expand Their Footprint

These factors allow me to seamlessly coordinate a team of the best-of-the-best professionals in the country. I start by personally working to understand the family on a much deeper level than what most professionals do by going into my discovery process with the "professional ignorance," or uber-objectivity, I mentioned above. That helps me understand which professionals the client has in place and then coordinate with those professionals and the right mix of people from my cohesive team of specialists and extended network to identify a number of high-performing alternatives.

Then, I help the business owner, and often the family, understand their options so they can make the best decisions. That level of coordination is the secret sauce that allows all of this to work. As you'll learn later in my book, my DMMFO model also requires the experts to be best-of-the-best, change their compensation structure to a value-only model, and a few other requirements. But for this to work, they all need to be well coordinated and willing to be part of a team, working seamlessly together to make sure the client's best interests are served. This level of coordination makes sure everyone is on the same page and each professional suggests potential solutions that fit within the client's bigger picture. Otherwise, a potential "solution" could create even bigger problems for the client than the challenge their solution intended to solve.

This quarterbacking and coordination is important because, in the final analysis, serving clients all falls back to the family making informed decisions for their future. For example, Russ Alan Prince, a key member of my core team who I will introduce to you in chapter 6, was recently working with a billionaire. While discussing various options, the billionaire asked Russ, "If you had my money, what would you do?" While understandable to ask, Russ was careful to redirect the conversation back to what the client wanted, replying:

> If I had your money, I wouldn't be talking to you, or anybody
> else. I'd build a castle on an island with a moat and make sure I
> was left alone. That would be the ideal lifestyle for me. But that
> might make you miserable, so let's focus on your life and the out-

comes *you* want to achieve. It doesn't matter what I would do. What really matters is what's best for you, your family, and your business. So let's talk through how each of the different possibilities affects your life. Then you'll be able to choose the possibility that will work best for what you want to achieve.

That's an important focus. There's a lot of complexity in many middle-market businesses. There are a lot of issues even beyond the business. There are the family dynamics that complicate everyone's lives. Even small differences between businesses or family dynamics make a big difference in what's best for each client.

That's why my cohesive team of specialists and I start with engaging in a detailed discovery process before we present any possible solutions. I learn what you want, filter various potential solutions through what I learn, then present you with the pros and cons of each option, so you can make an informed decision.

Gaps and Holes

Just about every business—even the ultra-successful—has gaps and holes. They might be different gaps and holes, but they almost all have them.

What happens is a lot of what people do: they do piecemeal. For example, so they did some wealth planning over here. Then someone else comes in and does some more wealth planning with them. Then someone else comes in and does some more wealth planning. Different specialties. Different focuses. Different products. One mess.

They end up with a bunch of disjointed plans or products. The professionals each put the business owner into the product the professional sells that they believe helps the company of the family in some way. But that piecemeal approach leaves the business owner without the most valuable piece of the process: a single, cohesive set of solutions that helps the business owners and the family optimally. These professionals sort of throw things at them like tossing spaghetti at the wall hoping something sticks.

This happens at the highest levels of wealth, all the way up to billionaires, when they don't have an expert truly operating with a family office approach and overseeing a well-coordinated team of specialists.

A lot of this goes on, and it goes on everywhere. For example, some lawyers—not all lawyers by any stretch of the imagination—but some lawyers have a standard formula they apply for when children will get money and how much money they will get at different ages. While it sounds great and fair on the surface, I have found that rigidly following that formula without concern for the specific children involved could cause tremendous harm to some of those children. In some cases, when I get to know the family members, I learn there are children whom the parents wouldn't trust with having access to money based solely on their age.

For example, what if one child is struggling with drugs? What if one has a gambling problem? Distributing money based solely on age could destroy these children's lives while draining the wealth that the parents worked hard for decades to accumulate. Families need someone in their corner who understands the family's dynamics and can shift through the options based on the family's unique needs and wishes.

Too many so-called "professionals" pay little attention to the real agenda of their clients: the needs, wants, desires, wishes, and concerns of their clients or the real-world concerns of the successful middle-market business owner. There are always going to be gaps with a piecemeal approach. There are always going to be problems.

Even with the best professionals and most well-conceived investment and wealth plans, life changes and plans become obsolete. They become dated. The solutions can get dated, and few business owners make the necessary revisions. The world changes, but not everyone stays current. For example, when we went through the whole crisis with COVID-19, some business owners were hurt by this and others did extremely well. Either way, most of those business owners didn't update their estate plans.

They'll get around to it. They are stuck in their business. But when you have $10 million or more in net worth, you might find yourself overleveraged in one area.

Three Qualities a Professional Needs Before Joining My DiNuzzo Middle-Market Family Office™ Team

As my DMMFO evolved as part of the natural extension of my Wealth Management practice, and as I helped my clients grow their wealth, I realized that my DMMFO can only work if everyone on my cohesive team shares three qualities: (1) they need to be among the most experienced and sophisticated professionals in their respective fields, (2) they need to be comfortable with a value-based compensation model where professionals are paid only when they provide exceptional value to a client, and (3) most importantly, they need to unequivocally understand I put my clients first before anyone else including myself.

With respect to the first quality, for a professional to join my DMMFO team, they must be among the best-of-the-best specialists in their field. They need to be recognized as such by their peers and other professionals in aligned fields. They need to be able to adroitly connect high-quality solutions to the array of issues that even many very experienced professionals miss. And their area of expertise needs to be in a field that impacts middle-market business owners.

Some of these professionals are specialists in a subject matter that comes up on a regular basis, such as personal tax mitigation. Others are specialists in subjects that come up less frequently, such as once a year or every other year or one time only such as buying an island. Professionals don't achieve this level of sophistication easily. They achieve this level of sophistication by working with middle-market business owners on complex issues over a long period of time.

With respect to the value-focused compensation model, I require that these professionals get out of the mindset of time-based billing. So a bill is not sent for every email, phone call, or passing thought that enters their mind about a client. People are rightfully frustrated when they get a bill for $500, or more, just for calling their attorney to ask a quick question. The DMMFO model works differently to be able to make the best-of-the-best specialists available to middle-market business owners and wealthy families.

In addition, the professionals need to be comfortable not making any money when their product or service isn't the right fit for the client or if the client chooses another option. The DMMFO doesn't operate like many professionals who walk into every meeting determined to present their products and services as the solution to every problem the client brings up. Instead, I tend to offer multiple viable options to my business owner and affluent family clients and explain the pros and cons of each choice to them.

The specialists on my cohesive team are comfortable knowing that their solutions won't always be an option I consider appropriate for my DMMFO clients. They also need to appreciate that their product or service won't be the only option I present to my clients. At DMMFO, the client comes first—always. Always has. Always will. Since 1989. This is the third quality and actually the first one I consider before bringing a specialist onto my cohesive team. Finally, they need to understand that the ultimate decision about which product or service my client will use rests with my client, and they only make money when the client chooses to move forward with their product or service.

Together, these three qualities are foundational and make the entire DMMFO process work. To qualify as a member of my cohesive team, professionals need to have *all three* qualities. No exceptions. Here's more about why each is so important to making the DMMFO process work.

There's No Substitute for Caring, Sophistication, and Experience among Well-Coordinated Specialists

While many professionals say they're client-centered, this is typically not the case. What I regularly find that sets DMMFO apart from the morass of professionals is that I and everyone on my cohesive team sincerely cares. We care about the well-being of all the middle-market business owners and successful families we work with. We care about helping them achieve their hopes and dreams as well as finding the best way to deal with their problems and concerns. We care about getting them the results they need and want.

Our caring is seen in our deep concern for our clients, but it's more than that. Our caring is operationalized as we put the financial interests of our clients above our own and above the specialists we bring to the table. What's best for the client is always what matters most.

At the same time, there's no substitute for sophistication and experience when working with middle-market business owners. It doesn't matter how hard someone works or how well-intentioned they are if they simply don't know where to look, what questions to ask, and what solutions are available.

An inexperienced accountant could have the best intentions but won't be able to structure the most tax-favored transaction if they don't know all the available options. An experienced estate planning attorney who works almost exclusively creating simple wills could cause you to pay millions of dollars in unnecessary estate taxes simply because they have never put together sophisticated estate plans involving trusts in multiple jurisdictions. Not all professionals are equally competent. In this context, working with the wrong professional can cause you a lot of harm, even if they have the best intentions.

With few exceptions, my middle-market business owner clients have come to me with professionals already in place. Often they have been working with an attorney, an accountant, or a trusted insurance professional for years. Yet almost without exception, in my initial conversations with them—the discovery process—I find that many of my clients have lived for years with dangerous risks and costly missed opportunities.

This happens for many reasons, but it all boils down to knowledge and experience. When these types of clients come to me, they generally either manage a group of professionals themselves or they have a trusted attorney, accountant, or insurance professional who has worked with them for a number of years.

In these situations, the business owner generally directs the professionals. That means they only get an estate plan if they request one, or they only evaluate their insurance and other risk management tools if they initiate it. Even then, the professionals they use are often either less sophisticated than they need to be or they're salespeople.

Contrast that with how my team and I work. We have spent decades working with successful middle-market business owners. I have personally been doing so since 1989. Each of us specializes in our areas of focus. We have access to dozens of strategies and tools and have used each of them many times. That gives us a unique ability to identify both the gaps and the opportunities for my clients. We know where to look to spot gaps and opportunities. We know what to look for. We know what questions to ask. We know how to close gaps and take advantage of all opportunities available to my clients. Finally, we know how often we need to revisit certain areas of my clients' lives to continue to optimize their affairs. That's what we do. In fact, that's all we do. All day, every day, we optimize my clients' businesses, families, philanthropy, and futures. And with my coordinating everyone so all professionals know what the others are doing and how they are adding value, we are able to help the client achieve much better results for their business, their families, and themselves.

It's not the business owner's fault. It's not fair to expect them to be able to manage sophisticated business strategies, family issues, philanthropy efforts, and other issues relating to their future while running their complicated business. It's not reasonable to expect them to be able to spot sophisticated legal, accounting, tax, health, and lifestyle topics my cohesive team of specialists and I have spent decades learning. They know what they know—inside and out—their business. I know what I know—how to help middle-market business owners optimize their lives.

The same is true with less sophisticated professionals. They don't have the same experience or level of expertise as professionals who have built their specialty after decades of working on the most sophisticated and complex projects. Thus, it doesn't matter how well-intentioned they are, they don't know what they don't know and routinely fail to spot the critical nuances that specialists like my team members do. As a result, their clients suffer either by being exposed to unnecessary risks, missing out on substantial opportunities available to them, or both.

My business owner clients get the best results when they can focus on doing what they do best—running their businesses and enjoying their lives at home—knowing they have a well-coordinated team of experienced specialists doing what we do best—helping them achieve their goals so they can continue to grow.

How My DiNuzzo Middle-Market Family Office™ Model Ties It All Together

I was recently talking with the senior partner of a mid-tier accounting firm about the process I use to coordinate the best-of-the-best professionals to serve middle-market business owners. The firm is very well respected. He had all the experience and sophistication to serve successful middle-market business owners and wealthy families well.

But as the discussion started touching on whether he might be a good addition to the team, I quickly realized he wouldn't make the cut. Why? Because sophistication and experience are only two of the factors needed to make this work. In addition to sophistication and experience, professionals need to buy into the way I structure our relationships with each other and the clients.

Specifically, every expert on my cohesive team needs to be willing to adjust the way they charge clients to only get paid when a client chooses a solution they help implement. If they propose an option, but the client chooses a different option, they don't get paid. When they do charge, they need to be willing to accept noncontingent, project-fee or value-fee billing, getting paid a set amount based on the value the client receives, even if that results in them getting paid a lower effective hourly rate than they typically charge. That said, there are limited scenarios where charging an hourly rate is the most appropriate.

Additionally, every expert on my cohesive team needs to work seamlessly with professionals from outside of their organization. I put the best team on each project. That can require an accountant from one firm working with a lawyer from another firm and an insurance specialist from a third firm. These professionals need to communicate and collaborate with each other so as to create the greatest value for the client. They need to play well together and check their egos at the door. And they need to understand that sometimes they will get paid and sometimes they won't, but in the long run, when we serve clients well, it works out for everyone.

This guy's firm could not (or *would* not) work that way, so their partner didn't make the cut.

First, they only bill hourly. If it takes them three hours to write a letter on behalf of the client, they bill the client for three hours of work. If the client calls them for 8 minutes, firms like theirs bill the client for 12 or even 15 minutes. While that offers some predictability on the firm's side, that mindset puts the client in an awkward position of not wanting to reach out for guidance with what they believe to be quick questions because they don't want to get billed to death. So they write the letter themselves or make the "small decision" on their own, often with limited information and amid all the chaos of running their businesses and managing their lives. Those decisions can cause big problems for the client in the long term in ways the client doesn't anticipate because they don't have all the necessary information before making the decision.

Contrast that with my model, which typically sets fees based on projects and value. My clients don't hesitate to call me with those "quick questions" because they know they can get an answer without an invoice. Sometimes that answer is truly a quick one. Other times, the client learns that the question might be a quick one, but the issue is not simple and requires me to do some homework. Collectively, my team has saved clients millions of dollars helping them answer "quick questions" that would never have been asked if we operated in the old, hourly based model.

To be clear, the old model isn't "bad" or "wrong"; it just doesn't work if you want to bring single-family-office-level service and expertise to middle-market business owners and wealthy families. The fact that this firm just bills hourly doesn't lend itself to the approach we're talking about. But there's nothing I can do to change it. The last thing I want to do is spend years trying to convince them to change how they have operated for decades. Instead, I find exceptional professionals who truly get it, value it, and want to build long-term value and relationships with middle-market business owners and affluent families. If I have to convince someone of the model, I move on. It has to work for everybody. So I find experts who are confident in the value of their expertise and comfortable being paid solely on a project or value-provided basis. And many of the best-of-the-best experts have that confidence.

In talking to lots of professionals, I've discovered that many of them want to have the same type of relationship as we have with our clients, but they don't want to adjust the compensation model. But the compensation model is a key reason why this works so well. And that involves providing expert advice at the highest level and, in the beginning of these engagements, not being paid because we need to let the client understand some of the basics before we can move forward.

That's very uncomfortable for many professionals. They ask, "What do you mean I'm going to give away my expertise and not be paid?" I answer, "Yes, that's what you're going to do. And when we find the right opportunity where we really can add value and make that difference, then we make money." It works because we get paid when we provide value to clients and that's it. We will be compensated but not because we spent 3 hours or 33 hours with a client. We are compensated when (and because) the solutions we offer provide an enormous multiple of value to our clients than the cost they incur for the analysis, advice, and recommendations. It's almost like a guaranteed value delivery when we do anything a client is expected to pay for.

Some professionals don't get it. Others do. And only the ones who get it and have the substantive experience and expertise to serve middle-market business owners and wealthy families well make it onto my cohesive team.

In the end, with the DMMFO, clients experience a value to cost dynamic where the value they receive is a multiple of any costs incurred. I'm not talking two or three times more either. I'm talking 5, 10, and sometimes even greater value received by the middle-market business owner or affluent family. It's not uncommon for a client to pay a one-time fee of $30,000 or $50,000 to save more than $500,000 in income taxes *a year—year after year.* This type of value proposition happens across many disciplines too.

Giving You Access to Unlimited Solutions

The other problem with the old way is how limited your options are when working with individual professionals.

As I mentioned earlier, the forgotten demographic typically works with one or more professionals with whom they've worked for many years, either solo professionals, small group practices, or people associated with a larger firm. This limits the solutions that the client is able to access to whatever the professional or their firm knows about (or sells).

Many times, this limitation is done without bad intent. The professional doesn't know all the possible solutions and doesn't have a high-quality extensive team of professionals to collaborate with like I do. A small percentage of the time, the firm only offers products or services that earn them high commissions or inflated fees or large hourly calculated invoices. They may know the client has other options but, if they are aware of these other prospective solutions, that would require them to refer the relationship to another professional and risk losing both short-term and long-term revenue.

So they don't offer anything they either don't know about or don't sell. All roads lead to the products and services that fit their model and benefit them. Some of even the smartest and most specialized professionals are stuck in a business model that works this way. And that means they don't make the best recommendations because they're trapped in their business model. Many advisors who have been working with successful business owner clients take this a step further. They don't want their successful business owner clients to "see the light of day" and talk with another advisor, even if that advisor is a specialist in a field that is not in competition with them. They get defensive and fear being threatened or embarrassed by the other professional.

The business model determines how they're compensated, what they're comfortable doing, and the way they're comfortable doing it. But that doesn't mean it is ideal for the middle-market business owner client—and the client should not have to limit their business, family, financial, and philanthropic future because hitting their goals doesn't fit into their professionals' business model. Your advisors should produce the best results for you. And that's what makes my middle-market family office model so valuable for successful business owners. My team of leading experts not only has the substantive expertise but they are also willing to adjust their compensation arrangements so it really works for you, the client. In the end, this results in a situation in which everybody comes out winning.

When an issue comes up, I can reach out to the appropriate key members of my cohesive team to begin gathering options and discerning possible high-impact solutions for my clients. Based on my in-depth understanding of the needs and concerns of the client, I can work with the appropriate professionals to whittle down the options to the best ones, and then we present them to the client. That means I'm not limited by what any single expert knows or sells—even though my team members are the best-of-the-best in their expertise and experience. I can pull from every available option to present my clients with the absolute best options from the best-of-the-best experts.

We Customize Solutions for You and Your Family

In addition to being able to recommend unlimited solutions and services, my DMMFO model also provides a deeper level of customization than what the forgotten demographic is used to. When your professionals are limited by their experience, specialization, and business model, you typically end up with cookie-cutter recommendations or recommendations that are only minimally customized. For example, an Investment Advisor might recommend investment choices that are less volatile because you are getting older or have a low risk tolerance. But their investment recommendations are limited because they either don't know about all available offers or only make money by offering a small selection of investment options.

With my DMMFO model, I can offer fully customized recommendations from an extensive pool of possible high-impact solutions so I can match our recommendations to your needs and even your personality. To match your personality as well as your needs, I use a methodology that helps us gain a much deeper understanding of you and your motivations than what we would learn from a simple risk profile. And because we can recommend everything that is legally possible, we can recommend options that precisely fit both your goals and your personality.

I also revisit your motivations as your life changes. I know your primary motivations shift along with your needs and goals as children or grandchildren are born, family moves away, you get older, and other changes occur in your life. I understand that world events and other factors also shift your priorities. I also know that spouses and other people of importance might differ with respect to priorities, motivations, and risk tolerance.

My discovery process takes all of this into account to understand each key family member's goals, motivations, and personality. One common example, as you might imagine, many times involves a wife and husband who have different goals, motivations, and personalities. In these cases, I work to understand each spouse so we can provide the best possible solutions. But, as appropriate, we also work with the couple through a joint "collective" or "couple's" goals, motivations, and personality exercise. This exercise helps us make even better recommendations for the family because I can point out the pros and cons of each possibility within the context of each person's motivations as well as what the couple has decided together.

For example, let's assume one spouse identifies income security, work-life balance, and asset protection as primary motivations, and the other spouse identifies growth of wealth, spending time with family, and leaving a legacy. Together, that couple might agree that, of those six motivations, their top three as a couple include income security, asset protection, and spending time with family (which would inevitably cause a better work-life balance).

Let's also assume the couple and I agree that (1) they are paying way too much in income taxes, and (2) their business could be providing more cash flow than it has been.

In this case, knowing their individual and "couple" motivations, I would bring together several members of my cohesive team to coordinate and discuss their individual and collective motivations and ask them to recommend ways to reduce income taxes and provide significantly more cash flow from the business.

Because the couple includes work-life balance and spending time with family in both their individual and collective motivations, my team and I would focus on solutions for improving cash flow that would not require more time from whoever is working in the business. Indeed, I would focus on options that would allow the couple to spend less time in the business while generating more (and more stable) cash flow. And I would make sure we would not recommend options that would take cash away from the business that it needs to operate.

In the end, each recommendation I make would be filtered through the client's goals, motivations, and personalities.

I can provide single-family-office-level value to the forgotten demographic because I work to understand my middle-market business owner and affluent family clients deeply and make sure my cohesive team understands each client's goals, motivations, and personalities as well. That information gives us a really effective way to get every member of my team completely aligned with each client.

We Change How Clients Perceive Professionals

Because of the nature of how I operate, many clients stop looking at us as a cost center. When they learn everything I do and how I structure the relationship, they realize it can be a *profit center*. That is regularly true with the billionaires who set up their own private offices, and it's true with the forgotten demographic I serve through my DMMFO.

My clients believe that their relationship with me will provide a net positive. It's not a "cost of doing business." It's not a "loss leader." It's truly a relationship they know will provide a substantial return, not just in terms of the financial benefits but also with respect to family, health, and lifestyle goals.

In the end, many of my clients begin to view their relationship with the DMMFO as the second most important contributor to their family's wealth and other goals—second only to the core business that helped them build the wealth in the first place.

They see their core business as what really drives their wealth building. But the DMMFO helps them optimize that wealth and use the advice and experience of the cohesive team to achieve goals well beyond their business.

Keys to Chapter

- From working with thousands of business owners, my team and I have learned that most professionals never develop a clue which strategy is truly best for their clients because they don't invest the time in talking to them to really understand all the issues involved.

- The better way is to—when possible—present multiple options to the family, along with the pros and cons of each, all framed within the context of that family's needs and goals. This starts with my thorough discovery process, through which I personally work to understand the family on a much deeper level than what most professionals do. That commonly enables me to understand which professionals the client has in place and then coordinate with those professionals and the right mix of people from my cohesive team of experts and extended network to identify a number of high-performing alternatives.

- This coordination is important because, in the final analysis, serving clients all falls back to the family making informed decisions for their future.

- My DiNuzzo Middle-Market Family Office can only work if everyone on the team shares three qualities: (1) they need to be among the most experienced and sophisticated professionals in their respective fields, (2) they need to be comfortable with a value-based compensation model where professionals are paid only when they provide exceptional value to a client, and (3) most importantly, they need to unequivocally understand I put my clients first before anyone else including myself.

- In the end, this allows us to recommend unlimited solutions, all customized to each client's goals, motivations, and personality.

PART 3:

———

How the DiNuzzo Middle-Market Family Office™ Helps Successful Middle-Market Business Owners

———

Chapter 6

How Engaging the DiNuzzo Middle-Market Family Office™ Can Be a Life-Changing Event *for the Forgotten Demographic*

As I've mentioned before, what makes my DiNuzzo Middle-Market Family Office™ method so valuable to my clients is that it brings together the right mix of the best-of-the-best experts with a singular focus of helping clients fill any gaps left open by their current mix of advisors in order to help them achieve their goals.

The concept of filling the gaps left open by their advisors is important. Some clients have one or more professionals in place who do a great job and bring valuable experience and knowledge to the table. In those instances, I work very well with those professionals and only bring others to the table with expertise and experience that the existing professionals lack. I piggyback on top of them, not work in lieu of them. You don't get to a certain level of success without *somebody* you can trust, even if they are not the best-of-the-best in their field. That's where I can come in to help.

Other clients don't have any professionals working with them and need me to bring in members from my team and network for any area of focus needed to help the clients achieve their goals. No matter what the client has in place, my goal remains the same: to bring to the table experts needed to help my clients achieve their goals.

In the end, my goal with my DMMFO is to help you avoid costly gaps and unlock opportunities you and your existing advisors have not yet taken advantage of. In fact, one of my colleagues who refers clients to me has described what I do as "printing money." "Do you want P. J. to print money for you?" he asks when describing my DMMFO. "Let him look around. He will find money for you. He's like a metaphorical printing press. You'll have a large stack of money once he gets rolling."

For many clients, that begins with my discovery process, undertaken by me and often one of my key specialists, such as family office expert Russ Alan Prince. Some of the wealthiest and most influential international, as well as national, families turn to Russ when they need help. He is a Visiting Scholar at the Forbes School of Business and Technology and is the author or coauthor of more than 60 books, including *Everyone Wins! How You Can Enhance and Optimize Business Relationships Just Like Ultra-Wealthy Entrepreneurs* and *How to Build a High-Performing Single-Family Office: Guidelines for Family Members and Senior Executives.*

Collectively, the cache of research-based insights within Russ's publications is the most complete empirical analysis in the field and the largest, most comprehensive database on the topic. And he's a key advisor at the DMMFO, helping me ensure each of my clients gets a full and true family office experience, just like the ultra-wealthy.

How Family Office Expert and Specialist Russ Alan Prince Helps Change the Lives of Clients, Their Families, and Their Businesses

Russ and I work closely together to set the tone for my clients through impactful listening. Like all members of my cohesive team of specialists, Russ is empathetic with high-net-worth clients and understands their unique needs. Whether it involves something as common as protecting assets, saving taxes, or improving their business, or something as nuanced as helping a family member tax efficiently immigrate to the U.S., Russ has seen it all.

In addition to his direct role in helping my middle-market business owner and affluent family clients achieve their unique goals and address their most pressing concerns, Russ uses his extensive connections throughout the Single Family Office world to help me identify additional professionals to consider for my cohesive team and extended network. He is especially adept at knowing exactly who to call for even the most nuanced and esoteric needs (such as when a wealthy family needed the services of a cryptozoologist or wanted a dollhouse designed by an internationally renowned architect).

Like me and all members of my cohesive team, Russ knows that he doesn't have all the answers. He is well aware of his limitations. He also knows our core team members might not even have all the answers. But, like me, he knows who to call to get any answers we may need to help our clients achieve their goals and address their concerns.

Russ is also committed to continuous learning and improvement and making sure we adapt as our clients' needs and wants change. He understands that the tools we use to help our middle-market business owner and affluent family clients achieve their agendas need to change along with the ever-changing political, social, and legal landscapes. Thus, he helps me ensure that my cohesive team is well coordinated and stays at the forefront of the issues that impact my clients.

My DMMFO Is Designed to Provide Unparalleled Service

As discussed in part 1, the existing wealth management world creates two classes of service: one for the ultra-wealthy and another for everyone else. It doesn't matter that you may have the same needs as the ultra-wealthy do. You can either afford and justify the expense of setting up a Single Family Office or you're likely to be thrown to the wolves to navigate the Private Wealth Hierarchy on your own.

With those choices, most successful business owners I come across end up in one of three situations.

First, they end up working with professionals who are vastly underqualified. They've outgrown their professionals' levels of experience and expertise. They're trustworthy but are not serving them well. (Some of them were in way over their head from the start.) This sets up the client for unnecessary catastrophe between gaps in protections and lost opportunities, especially because many people don't appreciate that I can work very well with existing trustworthy professionals. I bring in existing trusted professionals to the team serving my clients all the time with great success.

Second, they end up being sold to by a salesperson disguised as an advisor. This typically ends up with the clients being only slightly better off than if they were working with an underqualified professional. They often get some benefit from the product they purchase from the salesperson… but it's often not the *right* product, hardly ever the *best* product—and, to add insult to injury, the product rarely fits into the big picture of helping the client achieve their goals. There's almost always a better (and more affordable) option for the client.

Third, they end up having one large wealth management firm advising them. This typically ends up better for the client than either of the other two options, but it's still often far less than ideal. Generally speaking, the client ends up being placed into products or services the firm offers in-house. These advisors are typically mandated to exclusively use other in-house employees. Although these firms tend to have more options than the salesperson, these options are still limited and often costly. These firms cannot compare with the level of service capabilities and independence provided by the DMMFO.

With the variety of advisors needed to optimize your business, family, financial, and philanthropic lives, there's simply no way one organization can have the best-of-the-best professionals in every specialty. For that to be true, you would have to believe that the best-of-the-best professionals all want to be associated with one brand and live only in locations where that brand has offices. I've searched the entire country and beyond to find the best-of-the-best professionals in the specialties needed to serve you well. I assure you, they're not all in one place and don't all want to be associated with one brand.

I designed my DMMFO to serve you using only exceptional leading experts that fill needs that your current professionals cannot no matter where they live or what organization they're associated with. I hand-selected and vetted them to ensure they share the right client-first mindset with me and are willing to put their money where their mouth is by only charging clients when they add value. When I identify the right candidates for core areas of specialty that my clients generally need, I invite them to join my primary cohesive team. I also continue to search for additional specialists with the same mindset and commitment to include in my supporting network for those special needs that come up once every year or two.

Together, there's no issue for which my team and I can't call upon an expert with a client-first mentality to help you well. We're not beholden to one company, one solution, or even one brand of products or services. We're only beholden to you.

The Choice is Yours

Between me, my senior specialists like Russ, my cohesive team, and my extended network, there is simply no challenge we can't help you address in a compliant, aboveboard way.

This level of specialty and commitment to your success means

- I don't cut corners—and neither does anyone on my team of specialists.
- I work well with any existing professionals who are already serving you well, using my team and extended network to fill in any gaps of expertise or experience.
- I provide the most appropriate high-impact solutions in each situation.
- I ensure you can make insightful and informed decisions by making certain you clearly understand the advantages and disadvantages of every viable high-impact solution I present.
- I don't even tiptoe near "gray areas" when it comes to legality and compliance as everything I put forth is a bright-line transaction.

- I aspire to give you complete peace of mind, unparalleled service, and the freedom to spend more quality time with your loved ones and more time to spend on improving your physical and mental wellness. To be truly fulfilled, you *have* to live a balanced life. My consultative approach and network of best-of-the-best specialists help me ensure that my clients can finally achieve a healthy balance where they can be fulfilled in the present while having complete peace of mind that their future is secure for themselves and their family members.

Unlike most professionals you have dealt with, I don't "sell" anything. What I do in my discovery process is 100 percent consultative, conducting a detailed inquiry to identify options to present to you, along with their pros and cons, to allow you to make an informed decision about what's best for you. Contrast this approach with the most common approach of pushing you toward a single product or service.

Why don't I just recommend the option we believe to be the best? Three reasons.

First, I know you are an expert at making decisions. You would not be as successful as you are if you were not a smart decision-maker. You have made thousands of good decisions. If I can give you enough information about each of your options to make informed choices, I know you can make the best decision for your situation.

Second, as much as I learn about you, your family, your business, and your goals, you know yourself, your business, and your family members better than anyone else. The depth of knowledge I learn through my discovery process helps us recommend options that would meaningfully help you achieve your goals. But you are in the best position to make the final decision, as long as you have the information you need to make an informed choice.

Third, I want you to understand what you have in place and why. If you know what you have in place and why, you'll be much better at understanding when you need to update or change something. Way too many people hold on to outdated and ineffectual insurance policies, risk strategies, estate plans, and investments for far too long. If you ask them to explain why they have those policies, plans, or investments, their only answer is that their insurance agent, lawyer, or Investment Advisor recommended it years earlier.

Thus, I see my job as twofold. First, I don't ever tell you what to do. Instead, I learn everything I can about your goals and your unique situation. Second, I do research and present the best options to you, along with the pros and cons of each. That allows you to understand exactly what I suggest and why. It gives you everything you need to make informed decisions. And it helps you better understand when something might need to be updated or changed.

In the end, my DMMFO way can lead to much better results for you in both the short and long term.

Keys to Chapter

- My DiNuzzo Middle-Market Family Office provides best-of-the-best local, regional, national, and international experts on a value-driven compensation model to help the forgotten demographic achieve all their business, family, financial, and philanthropic goals.

- My team and I work closely with any of your trusted professionals already in place to fill in any gaps in experience or expertise needed to help you achieve your goals.

- I see my job as twofold. First, I don't ever tell you what to do. Instead, I learn everything I can about your goals and your unique situation. Second, I do research and present the best options to you, along with the pros and cons of each.

- Unlike most professionals you have dealt with, I don't "sell" anything. What I do in my discovery process is 100 percent consultative, conducting a detailed inquiry to identify options to present to you, along with their pros and cons, to allow you to make an informed decision about what's best for you.

- Between me, my key specialists such as Russ Alan Prince, my cohesive team, and my extended network, there is simply no challenge we can't help you address in a compliant, aboveboard way—even when faced with the most nuanced and esoteric needs (such as when a wealthy family needed the services of a cryptozoologist or wanted a dollhouse designed by an internationally renowned architect).

Chapter 7

Optimize Tax Advantages, Investment Outcomes, and Harmony with Your Personal Values Using Custom Indexing through Customized "Separately Managed Accounts"

When I started my firm in 1989, I was one of very few professionals in the Private Wealth industry who took a "goal-oriented" approach with my clients.

At the time, the vast majority of professionals basically searched for commissions and followed cookie-cutter formulas, telling their clients what to do with their money based on their age, income, and a few other factors. I, on the other hand, took a goal-oriented approach, taking the time to learn my clients' goals, risk tolerance, and other factors that would tell me the formulaic approach wasn't ideal.

As the years passed and my clients' balances grew, I was sure other industry professionals would catch on and adjust their approach. Unfortunately for them, very few did. To this day, only a small percentage of professionals take a truly customized approach to serving their clients. The formulaic (and, frankly, lazy) approach they take is "easier," so these so-called professionals convince their clients that their approach is the "conventional wisdom."

When I complete my discovery process, however, I frequently discover that these clients could achieve significant benefits by using a sophisticated investment tool, which I refer to as "Custom Indexing," which requires access to and understanding of "Separately Managed Accounts," or Custom SMAs.

Not surprisingly, very few of my clients have even heard of Custom Indexing or Custom SMAs before they work with me. Only a very small percentage of wealth management professionals know what they are. Fewer have access to the tools needed to properly structure them. And even *fewer* have the experience and sophistication to use them to their full advantage. Custom SMAs require extremely sophisticated software, to which many professionals don't have access, and expert data analysis, which many so-called professionals are unable or unwilling to perform.

In this chapter, I will introduce just some of the benefits of Custom Indexing and Custom SMAs and how I use them to help DMMFO clients reduce taxes and achieve better and more customized investment results.

Using Separately Managed Accounts to Create Custom Index Funds

From time to time, advances in the investment industry create formerly unheard of opportunities for investors. For example, Mutual Funds allow investors to spread investment risk across hundreds of securities with minimal funds. Additionally, Exchange Traded Funds, or ETFs, allow people to trade in and out of baskets of securities, achieve leveraged results, and more, with ease. More recently, Separately Managed Accounts, or Custom SMAs, help the right investors to achieve better investment objectives and results by creating Custom Index Funds built around what matters most to the investor.

In simple terms, Custom SMAs allow investors to hold a large basket of stocks that can be managed by a professional on their behalf, typically a registered Investment Advisor like me. They act similar to Mutual Funds and ETFs but with much more flexibility and several key differences.

Those differences allow investors to achieve much more control over their investment and even create *Custom* Index Funds, which I will discuss in more detail below.

Contrast that with how the typical Mutual Fund works. Mutual Funds and ETFs don't take your values into account when choosing investments, and they operate under strict rules. They need to invest in specific securities. They need to rebalance at specific times. They operate under a cloak of secrecy, making identifying what securities you are investing in through the fund impossible. You buy a fund, and the fund invests on your behalf in a completely off-the-shelf, one-size-fits-all fashion that is dictated by the fund documents and fund manager desires.

Until Custom SMAs were created, achieving more customized results was virtually impossible. However, as technology advanced, the most sophisticated Private Wealth Professionals became able to finally help you take complete control over—and achieve full transparency with—your investments through Custom Indexing. As discussed below, Custom Indexing technology allows me to put *you* in the driver's seat for your investments. You get to decide the methodology through which your own custom Mutual Fund operates. You can decide to shift the methodology as your needs or priorities change in life. And you get to achieve better, more customized results, with several additional advantages such as zero trading commissions, options for fractional share investing, sophisticated tax-loss harvesting, values-based investing, factor tilts, and more.

Custom Indexing: Creating Your Own Custom Mutual Fund

Many professionals on the Private Wealth Hierarchy convince their clients that standard Mutual Funds or ETFs are the best way to build a portfolio of publicly traded securities. They explain that this is the "conventional wisdom" in the industry and how people have made money for decades. While that might be true, it reveals an ignorant and lazy approach to serving clients. Those so-called professionals either don't know about Custom SMAs, don't have the ability to set up Custom SMAs, or don't want to do the work to set up and manage the Custom SMAs. They would rather just convince their clients to accept the lesser solutions of the "set-it-and-forget-it" Mutual Fund or ETF.

When it comes to Mutual Funds or ETFs, cookie-cutter funds typically are not the best fit. Specific goals, tax strategies, and even personal preferences will render off-the-shelf options inefficient or not ideal. In those cases, Custom Indexing might be a better option. For example, here are some of the advantages of Custom Indexing.

- Tax Optimization
- Investment Customization
- Custom Values-Based Investing (Environmental, Social, and/or Governance)
- Excluding Companies or Industry Sectors
- Sophisticated Research and Data Analysis
- Charitable Giving Strategies
- Custom Reporting
- Lower Costs
- Factor Tilts (Value, Small Cap, Profitability, Direct Investment)

Once you and I develop the criteria that matter to you, I research and present you with custom investment options to create your initial portfolio of investments in your Custom Index Fund. Think of this as me helping you create your own personal, highly customized Mutual Fund. I then monitor each of your investments to identify additional opportunities to enhance results, lower taxes, and otherwise achieve your goals.

Because Custom SMAs and Custom Indexing are so underutilized by Private Wealth professionals, below I will discuss some of the most common benefits of Custom Indexing in more detail.

Tax Optimization

Although the term "tax-loss harvesting" is commonly understood in the investment world, few professionals take full advantage of tax-loss harvesting capabilities. In a minority of cases, advisors review client portfolios at the end of each year to identify potential tax losses. If they find some, they might sell those securities to lock in those gains and then transfer those funds to another investment. While helpful, the process is inefficient at best and requires stocks to be down at one specific point in time. That leaves many opportunities for tax-loss harvesting lost, such as downturns earlier during a specific tax year.

With Custom SMAs and Custom Indexing, the software helps identify individual securities that will help us lock in tax losses year-round. Over the long term, locking in temporary losses can both enhance your returns and contribute significantly to your overall wealth building. You can lock in helpful tax losses by closing one position and moving those funds into a new position whenever you want. You have complete control.

With cookie-cutter Mutual Funds, you don't control when a fund manager closes a security. The only control you have is to sell the entire fund if it is down.

Additionally, Custom SMAs allow me to help reduce taxes in many circumstances, such as when a client inherits a portfolio of appreciated stocks. If the person inheriting the stocks has different investment goals and risk tolerance levels than the person who left the portfolio to them, they will typically want to change the investment mix. If done so independently, that would normally cause them to realize large capital gains. If they incorporate their inherited shares into a Custom SMA, I will have greater flexibility and can sometimes avoid realizing some or all of those capital gains. For example, if other stocks in their Custom Index Fund had similar investment profiles but a higher tax basis, I could sell those stocks instead of the inherited ones to end up in the same position but with a lower tax bill or no tax bill at all.

Sophisticated Charitable Giving Strategies

Custom Indexing allows you to achieve greater tax-advantaged charitable giving strategies by finding ways to donate appreciated individual securities. For example, some clients donate securities directly to a charity that's important to them. Others donate appreciated securities to a donor-advised fund that can distribute funds to multiple charities of the client's choice.

Combined with sophisticated tax-loss harvesting, charitable giving through donating appreciated securities offers an additional level of income tax savings.

Custom "Values-Based" Investing (Environmental, Social, and/or Governance)

Although "Value-Based Mutual Funds" have grown in popularity in recent years, what's important to you is different from what is important to others. Thus, cookie-cutter Value-Based Mutual Funds are not always the best option for a values-driven investor.

Custom Indexing provides much greater control and transparency with respect to environment, social, governance, and other important issues that matter to you. This includes specific issues such as companies tied to human trafficking, companies whose businesses violate specific religious values, and virtually any other issue that's important to you.

Using SMA software, I can research and filter every individual security and sector in your Custom Index Fund to include or exclude companies or sectors based on your goals and values.

You decide exactly what's in your portfolio.

Investing with Greater Transparency

When you invest in cookie-cutter Mutual Funds, you have no idea what your money is invested in. You can dig through quarterly reports to see a snapshot of the holdings at the end of the quarter. You can see the top 10 holdings using various websites, although that's not updated in real time either. But that's about it. You know the fund's purpose but have no idea what you actually own. And you can't access a list of transactions in real time either.

With Custom Indexing, you have complete transparency. You see exactly what your money is invested in at all times. You see everything. Every security. Every transaction.

Building a Better Portfolio through Custom Indexing and Custom SMAs

Custom Indexing and Custom SMAs give you complete control and transparency over your investments. Because of that, they have become one of the highest-impact tools in my toolbox through which many of my clients achieve better outcomes, save federal income taxes, and invest with greater peace of mind.

Keys to Chapter

- To this day, only a small percentage of professionals take a truly customized approach to serving their clients. The formulaic (and, frankly, lazy) approach they take is "easier," so these so-called professionals convince their clients that their approach is the "conventional wisdom."

- By taking a customized approach to helping my clients achieve their goals, I can build clients a Custom Index Fund using sophisticated Customized Separately Managed Account, or SMA, technology.

- Custom Indexing helps clients improve tax optimization, investment customization and control, custom values-based investing, charitable giving, factor tilts, and more.

- Very few of my clients have even heard of Custom Indexing or Custom SMAs before they work with me. Only a very small percentage of wealth management professionals know what they are. Fewer have access to the tools needed to properly structure them. And even *fewer* have the experience and sophistication to use them to their full advantage.

- Custom SMAs require extremely sophisticated software, to which many professionals don't have access, and expert data analysis, which many so-called professionals are unable or unwilling to perform.

Chapter 8

Using Sophisticated Strategies to Achieve Advanced Estate and Family Planning Goals

As my clients' needs grew, my need for more sophisticated and experienced experts grew as well. And because my DiNuzzo Middle-Market Family Office™ helps clients improve every area of their business and personal lives, I needed experts for every tool in my DMMFO toolbox, from investments to estate planning to family planning to risk management to sophisticated tax strategies, and more. You name it, only the best-of-the-best would make the cut. For several years, I scoured the country identifying, interviewing, and onboarding the best experts in the country in the most important areas to ensure my clients' success.

Over the next several chapters, I'll introduce you to some of the experts I have brought on my team to work alongside me as I help you achieve your goals. For example, one of my closest and most frequently used specialists is national and international family office expert and specialist Ed Renn, one of the most respected attorneys in the United States. From his New York City office, he advises some of the most successful businesspeople in the world. And he works closely alongside me to help my DMMFO clients achieve even the most complex estate, business, and family planning goals.

Ed was first admitted to practice law in 1988. Today, he is a principal at Withersworldwide, where he provides sophisticated legal advice on domestic and international estate planning, business succession, income maximization, and international tax planning to some of the most successful people in the world.

While he spends his days in Manhattan, communicating with colleagues in any of Withersworldwide's offices is just a phone call away for Ed. If his clients have an issue in Asia, he can call colleagues in Hong Kong, Singapore, or even Tokyo. If they run into a complex Italian legal issue, he can call colleagues in his firm's Milan office. With offices all around the U.S. and the world, Ed and his colleagues are able to handle even the most complex domestic or international legal challenge.

In addition to being an experienced, connected, sophisticated attorney, Ed is a creative problem solver and passionate about helping wealthy individuals grow and protect the businesses and income they worked so hard to build. It's that passion that attracted me to Ed when looking to build my core DMMFO team. But his experience and expertise alone were not enough for me to ask for him to be on my team. Ed needed to also buy into the value-first manner in which we operate instead of the traditional bill-for-all-time-worked model the legal industry typically operates. After all, a New York attorney with his experience and sophistication rightfully commands top rates for his time. But for my DMMFO model to work, the best-of-the-best specialists must commit to only benefiting financially when the benefit to my clients far exceeds their fees. And they need to be willing to work closely with me, any professionals that the client has in place who are serving the client well, and other professionals on my cohesive team of specialists, under my direction, in order to serve the client well.

Admittedly, this structure was a challenge when it came to many areas of the legal industry. Within the context of a middle-market family office model, however, I was sure we could find a way to make it work. Sure enough, Ed immediately understood the challenge I was working to overcome in order to give the same level of service he normally provided only to the ultra-wealthy to middle-market business owners and wealthy families.

Today, Ed is a core member of my cohesive team of specialists and works closely alongside me, other members of my cohesive team, my extended DMMFO network, and with many professionals the clients bring to the table to provide the most sophisticated services and benefits to clients all around the country.

How Family Office Expert and Specialist Attorney Ed Renn Helps Change the Lives of Clients, Their Families, and Their Businesses

While many of the benefits clients receive by having access to a well-coordinated team of specialists through the DMMFO can be measured on a balance sheet, income statement, or statement of net worth, some of the greatest and most impactful benefits clients experience because of our model never make their way to financial statements.

Take family and legacy planning, for example. Many clients I meet have no family or legacy planning in place. They have nothing. No will. No trust. No plan. Others have a basic plan in place that was created by a professional who followed a few formulas to put some basic estate and legacy planning together. The vast majority of those clients haven't reviewed or reconsidered their estate and legacy plan in years despite often dramatic changes in tax laws, family dynamics, and their business and financial standing.

While often better than nothing, basic estate and legacy planning can often result in devastating results for families. Take the most basic issue we uncover during our discovery process: a basic plan created based on "standard" formulas. These formulas encourage parents to leave assets in trust for their children or grandchildren. Those trusts often allow the assets to be liquidated for certain expenses, such as healthcare, education, or car or house purchases. Leftover funds are then generally released at intervals as the beneficiaries reach certain age thresholds, such as 21, 35, and 50 years of age.

When we review these plans with families, we almost always learn that the formula followed is not ideal for the family. Many times, we find that the formula followed could actually *harm* the children that the parents were trying to protect by setting up a trust.

For example, we often learn that one child has trouble managing money. Money that is released to them will immediately be squandered. Even worse, that child often uses the money to assume other obligations. They buy things on credit, or they buy assets that require ongoing maintenance or upkeep. Thus, if they were to receive a large sum of money, they would likely use it for a down payment on something but not have the money to make the ongoing monthly payments or address upkeep. Within months or years, they'd lose the asset or worse.

We also often learn that one child might have an alcohol, drug, or gambling problem. In these cases, releasing large sums of money based solely on their age could cause incredible harm. At best, the years of hard work that Mom and Dad invested in building their company to provide a better life for their children would be wasted as the children squander the money. At worst, in cases of children addicted to alcohol or drugs, it could kill them.

Unfortunately, many professionals don't think about life and legacy planning this way. They set it up based on a formula that appears "fair" on the surface but could have devastating results for the family.

Children squandering assets because they're distributed based on a formula is only one of many situations we uncover that could have unintended negative consequences for the family. Other common issues and concerns we discover that have not been addressed by less sophisticated advisors include the following:

- Plans not being revisited or updated after significant changes in laws.
- Plans not being revisited or updated after significant family changes, such as divorces, new marriages, new children, stepchildren, and even deaths.

- Plans not protecting family assets in the case of a child's death or divorce in the future, in this case being able to protect assets in the event the child does not enter into a prenuptial agreement.

When we get to the details of what our clients want for their families and what their existing plan (or lack thereof) would result for them, many of them become worried; some become angry. But the truth is, estate and legacy planning is part of our core business. We know the impact it can have on the clients we serve, so we hand-select the best-of-the-best specialists for our cohesive team, like Ed Renn, a principal at Withersworldwide who offers myriad legal advice for U.S. and international matters.

We designed our cohesive team to have all the right people at the table alongside me, like Ed Renn, so our clients can focus on what they do best and don't have to worry about the details when it comes to their estate and legacy plans. We know they have their own businesses to run and families to care for. So we can't expect them to know all the nuances of what's possible when less sophisticated professionals don't even know what's possible. Frankly, we can't even expect them to know what questions to ask their professionals when it comes to the intricacies of estate and legacy planning. It's our job as professionals to know what questions to ask our clients to get the information needed to help them achieve their goals. We also need to understand that our clients' life situations change frequently. And we need to understand that calling their estate and legacy planning specialist might not be top of mind when changes occur. So we also need to make sure we reconnect with them on a regular basis to ensure their existing plan is optimized for their current life circumstances.

This is where partners such as Ed Renn step in.

"There's a lot that clients would like to get done, and they're looking for assistance in organizing their thoughts and organizing their actions on what should happen first," says Ed. "A Middle-Market Family Office can certainly do that for clients."

Ed's expertise is of particular importance because new laws are being enacted all the time. Families can't just set it and forget it and expect the best results. This is especially true as I write this book while the Biden administration takes over the federal government. As we know, every four or eight years, priorities and philosophies can shift 180 degrees.

In this chapter, Ed walks us through how he works with people, and then discusses some of the advanced strategies he's used around estate planning and charitable trusts, among other topics.

Timeless and Valuable Engagement with Clients

As a core member of the DMMFO cohesive team, Ed engages with families by actively listening first. He's empathetic to the needs of ultra-high-net-worth clients. "They have significant assets and closely held businesses, and they're looking for tax savings for the family," he says. "It could be savings on the income tax side, on the estate and gifts tax side—transfer tax or income tax. It's all the same in money."

Ed reaches out for the best possible assistance whenever necessary. "I'm a huge believer in a team," he says. "I'm a huge believer that I don't have all the answers. The accountant doesn't have all the answers; the Financial Advisor doesn't have all the answers. But if the three of us come together and have a conversation, we're more powerful than we are individually."

When Ed engages with a new family that has, for example, just sold a business and is now worth $50 million, he sees so many opportunities, provided they work together and stay coordinated. "Some of the mistakes we sometimes see are the clients thinking lawyers are fungible—that any lawyer is going to produce the same document," says Ed. "The reality is, we all have our philosophies and underlying preferences. A suite of documents should reflect the philosophy with a consistent approach."

Ed and other partners of the DMMFO understand that the tools and strategies need to change along with the ever-changing political and legal landscapes. Instead of focusing on the tools and strategies, however, we dedicate our efforts to connecting our clients with the right experts, like Ed, who then help find and suggest high-impact solutions that can help our clients achieve their goals. Our team members give our clients multiple options, present the pros and cons of each, and then help our clients make informed decisions about what's best for them. After all, we know our clients are experts at making decisions. They have become successful in many facets of their lives by making thousands of good decisions. And they know themselves, their businesses, and their family members well. The depth of knowledge we learn through the DMMFO process helps us recommend multiple options that would help our clients achieve their goals. But we know that our clients are in the best position to make the final decision. And that leads to much better results for our clients in both the short and long term.

Estate Planning

By recruiting experts such as Ed, who works closely with me to ensure his work fits seamlessly within the big picture of each client's goals, DMMFO provides significant value for estate planning, whether it's starting from scratch or making the necessary adjustments to meet today's changing times and tax laws.

"The ones that are easiest to fix are the ones who have done very little," says Ed. "Usually if people have done a lot of planning, particularly if the planning hasn't been state of the art, it takes time and effort and costs to fix or undo what they've already done."

Ed shares a story of a family in the Midwest who, with his help, were able to turn their estate planning into a success story. When the father was in his late 70s with hundreds of millions of dollars of property, he turned to Ed. "With proper planning over the course of seven or eight years, Mom and Dad were able to transfer virtually all of that to the children, largely tax-free," says Ed, adding that the estate paid only $3 or $4 million in taxes over the course of both deaths. He's still working with all four of what was then the second generation and is now the first. "So we're doing the same thing for Generation Two that we did for Generation One," he says. "And a lot of what we did for Generation One still applies to Generation Two, but because of the magnitude of the wealth, we had both Generation-Skipping Trust, or GST, exempt trusts and nonexempt trusts." Ed is now planning with nonexempt trusts for the younger generation who are now in their 60s, and is "able to do some creative things for them" because of the successful planning approach.

How often do families review estate plans with specialists such as Ed? He presents three scenarios:

1. When they have a life-changing event, such as a death in the family; a birth, particularly a first birth for a couple that hasn't had children; and selling a business. "If you've got a situation where your executor, your trustee dies, or you're leaving a lot of money to your niece and you've decided your niece is unworthy, those are all reasons to call me and get the documents changed," says Ed.

2. Every five years, he does a "check-up" for most clients. "This makes sense because it accommodates a fair amount of law changes on the federal and state levels, both of which impact estate planning," says Ed.

3. Every two to three years for those who have a strong and growing income or wealth.

Ed brings up the example of clients who did their estate planning in 2016 and have found their world is very different now. "They were going through the documents, and they were shocked and horrified to see who they were benefiting," says Ed. "They didn't feel the same about these people today as they did five years ago."

In most cases, the estate planning foundation is fairly basic. "About 90 percent of the time plain vanilla is good enough," says Ed. "But the documents have to have the bells and whistles in them from the beginning because if something happens to you once you pass, you can't tell me, 'Gee, it would have been great if we would have had a power of attorney.' You need to build the documents with the idea that maybe you're not going to use this. But it's like the fire alarm in my house—I don't want to hear it go off, but I'm glad I have it."

Ed's office weaves safety nets under clients for many different potential problems, whether they're selling property and want to look at a

1031 exchange or have just written a best seller and can now tuck away $500,000 or more a year.

"Ultimately the estate planning document is a way you protect your spouse and your children," says Ed.

Foreign Grantor Trusts

For deferred compensation and asset protection, working with the DMMFO can provide significant inbound and outbound tax planning benefits.

"It's a huge win," says Ed, who encourages clients not born in the U.S. or who are not U.S. citizens to take advantage of foreign grantor trusts.

"Using a foreign grantor trust is absolutely the greatest trick in the bag," says Ed, explaining how clients can work with the DMMFO to transfer money with no income tax consequences to invest offshore. "Most offshore investors pay no income tax on capital gains on U.S. investment assets." As Ed continues, clients can invest offshore and immediately start making money through the life-changing services of the DMMFO.

How about inbound tax planning benefits? "In the last 10 years, the U.S. has become the new Switzerland," says Ed, adding how global transparency laws mean the U.S. does not share information with the U.K., China, and Singapore, among other countries. For those who aren't able to access foreign grantor trusts, the U.S. has been trending toward more affordable tax rates. Ed knows how to set up trust structures in states with no income tax.

"We can create a very nice benefit that could be dynastic and go on for 800 years or more," says Ed. "It's hard to know what that means because if you go back 800 years from now, we were talking about an agrarian, feudal world in which there were serfs—no banks, no equities." But the reality is, adds Ed, if families can allocate that generation-skipping transfer tax exemption that all U.S. taxpayers have, investments will also be GST exempt. "If you are very good at investing and if your children are prudent and frugal and don't spend a lot of money on planes and boats and big houses," says Ed, "you'll be able to move money down through three, four, or five generations without the confiscatory gift in the estate taxes kicking in—that's huge."

Charitable Trusts

As Ed explains, the DMMFO process can help families who want to make a philanthropic impact create a charitable lead trust in a simple, tax-favored way. On the surface, it's a fairly simple setup. But the magic is in the details, which Ed and others on the DMMFO cohesive team handle. "If clients give $1 million to a charitable lead trust, then they get an income tax dedication for $1 million," says Ed, who works hard to ensure clients don't give more to charity than they can deduct. The immediate deduction, he says, is great when a family has an unexpected windfall, or maybe has a junky piece of property and never could quite figure out what to do with it. If somebody came along and offered the family a price that would knock their socks off, they might figure, "Let's get rid of it now." But if you had a good year, and you don't need the income, a charitable lead trust could be the answer.

"Or maybe you're at a point in life where you're thinking about your charitable inclinations and your philanthropic goals," says Ed. "You can take a certain amount and put it into a charitable lead trust. You get the immediate tax deduction, which offsets the tax effect for having the income. The IRS says, 'Gee, what do we expect this thing to earn, so they look to interest rates.'" As of this writing, that would be about six-tenths of 1 percent, or a 60-basis point hurdle rate.

"You can do better than 60 basis points with an investment portfolio, so you can effectively earn mid-single-digit returns—7 or 8 percent," says Ed, who might advise a family in this situation to start out at the end of year one by giving a relatively small piece of the $1 million to charity. "The IRS says over the course of 15 years you have to transfer the $1 million plus this six-tenths of 1 percent growth rate to the charity," he explains. "So anything you earn beyond that six-tenths of 1 percent stays around, typically for your children, nieces and nephews, friends."

For families who want some flexibility because they're not sure what causes they're going to care about in 15 years in terms of their charitable interests, middle-market family offices can create flexibility by working with partners such as Ed. "It's not all hardwired that it has to go to the church or has to go to the alma mater," he says.

Charitable remainder trusts, Ed adds, tend to work better in higher interest rate environments. "But if we have significantly increasing interest for income tax rates or capital gain rates," he says, "we have a need for some shelter." And because successful professionals often have a big chunk of their net worth in IRAs and qualified plans, the DMMFO can help them leave those to charities, and leave other investments to their offspring."

 Keys to Chapter

- Many successful middle-market business owners have estate plans in place that do not adequately protect the family's assets or achieve the family's wishes. Many also don't have trusts in place to protect their assets and minimize tax obligations.

- New laws are being enacted all the time that impact trusts and estates. Families can't put an estate plan or trusts in place and expect the best results years down the road. Plans need to be revisited by experts after significant changes in laws and family changes, such as divorces, new marriages, new children, stepchildren, and even deaths.

- Estate plans also need to protect family assets in the case of a child's death or divorce in the future, in this case being able to protect assets in the event the child does not enter into a prenuptial agreement.

- The vast majority of estate planning attorneys don't have the experience and expertise necessary to help you optimize an estate plan.

- By recruiting experts such as attorney Ed Renn, who works closely with me to ensure his work fits seamlessly within the big picture of each client's goals, DMMFO provides significant value for estate planning and putting the right trusts in place to achieve your goals, whether it's starting from scratch or making the necessary adjustments to meet today's changing times and tax laws.

Chapter 9

Improve Results While Reducing Risk in Both Your Business and Personal Life

When your business and wealth grow, so does the complexity of your life. And that means risk. That's why I brought Clay Saftner onto my cohesive team of specialists. Clay Saftner is a principal and the chief operating officer of what I consider to be one of the top independent risk management firms between New York City and Chicago, Simpson McCrady. He's one of very few equity partners at the company, a firm with roots dating back more than 100 years. He's a national expert on all aspects of personal lines and commercial risk management and has helped me protect my clients from some of the most complex and sophisticated risk management issues you could imagine.

Simpson McCrady is headquartered in Pittsburgh, Pennsylvania, and is the largest Chubb insurance broker between New York City and Chicago helping people manage both business and personal risk. They have been awarded elite recognitions by some of the biggest and best insurance carriers around the country. For example, in 2005 Chubb created a program to recognize its most valued partners in the risk management world as "Cornerstone" agencies, a designation that has been awarded to only about

3 percent of Chubb appointed agencies or brokers. As you might imagine with such a small percentage of agencies qualifying for the recognition, Cornerstone agencies must demonstrate the highest performance metrics.

Not only did Simpson McCrady receive the highly prestigious recognition as a Cornerstone Agency the first year Chubb began issuing that recognition but it is also the only firm that has maintained that recognition for both private client and commercial insurance every year since. The recognition is not just an industry accolade either. It comes with several perks that Simpson McCrady can pass along to its clients, such as direct access to senior Chubb executives, 24-hour customer service, special claims contacts to ensure clients receive the most effective service in cases of loss, special coverage needs and exceptions, and more. The firm also maintains similarly prestigious and impactful designations with other well-recognized insurance companies as well.

Clay has decades of experience regarding both commercial property & casualty and personal lines insurance solving sophisticated and complex risk management challenges for literally thousands of clients in the U.S. and overseas. As part of my core team, he brings that experience and sophistication and those broad Simpson McCrady relationships to DMMFO clients. From the initial discovery process to changing circumstances and ongoing risk management assessments, Clay and I work closely together to identify risk and then create action plans to avoid, mitigate, transfer, or even knowingly accept those risks to help lead my clients closer to their goals.

How Risk Management Expert and Specialist Clay Saftner Helps Change the Lives of Clients, Their Families, and Their Businesses

Imagine you're sitting in your office after a busy day when your cell phone rings. It's a call you never wanted to receive. Your teenage son was in a horrible car accident in a car owned by you. He's expected to survive, but three other people weren't so lucky.

You spend the first several hours and days learning the details of the accident and dealing with the physical and emotional fallout. Your son let his friend drive your car. There was no driving under the influence. No drugs or alcohol at all. But the road was slick from a midafternoon thunderstorm, and the car hydroplaned and crashed. Months later, you're served with a lawsuit seeking more than $10 million in damages.

If this hypothetical sounds too specific to be made up, it's because it's not. This is a true situation from a client who had a proactive risk management plan in place that was designed by Clay and his colleagues at Simpson McCrady. Fortunately, while the real-world implications of the accident were horrific, Clay's risk management plan protected the CEO from financial implications through an insurance program that covered all costs of defending the lawsuit and the exposure from the liability to compensate the victims and their families.

Stories like this happen every day to successful business owners all around the world. But, many times, the business owners are surprised to learn they do not have the right risk management plan in place to limit or eliminate financial exposure. In fact, with so many assets being owned by companies but used for personal use, and vice versa, many business owners are shocked to learn how much their business and personal assets are truly exposed.

But that's where experts like Clay come in. As a core member of the DMMFO cohesive team of experts, Clay works closely with me, other professionals on my team, and any professionals my clients already have in place to make sure our clients are adequately protected against losses that occur in their business or personal lives. That way, when tragedy strikes—and it will in one way or another, and you call me to ask what you need to do—you can rest assured that your assets and financial future are protected and you can concentrate on what's most important in life.

Your Footer and Foundation for a Secure, Prosperous Present and Future

Clay joined my core team for one purpose: to help me provide you with a solid world-class foundation upon which to build a secure, prosperous present and future. And that starts with managing risk in such a way that also improves your results and delivers peace of mind.

For example, in the scenario above, had Clay and his colleagues not put in place a risk management plan for the CEO, one mistake could have wiped out $10 million or more in liability loss alone. The CEO might have had to sell a house, liquidate investments at a loss, or borrow millions of dollars to defend the lawsuit and satisfy any settlement or judgment.

Because the CEO had a robust risk management plan in place, however, he could focus on what really mattered without having to worry that the accident would financially wipe out what he had worked so hard to build.

I liken what Clay's risk management planning does for your present and your future to what a home inspector does before you purchase a home. Before you buy a home you intend to live in, you hire an expert to inspect it inside and out, top to bottom, and identify any flaws that need to be addressed. On even the smallest homes, inspections often identify dozens of issues that need to be addressed. Sometimes those issues are small. But other times, the inspector finds a crack in the foundation. Until the crack is repaired, the house is in danger. Repairing the foundation needs to be complete before almost anything else. After all, it doesn't matter how beautiful a new kitchen is if the foundation upon which it sits is crumbling.

Clay and I go through a similar discovery and risk management planning process for every client of DMMFO to achieve the same impact on your life that a home inspector can have on real property. We help you protect what you've built so you can confidently move forward without worrying that it will all come crashing down—just like the car accident didn't cause what the CEO had built to come crashing down.

Your risk management plan acts as the foundation of your world, and Clay and I make sure there are no cracks.

Risk Management and the Discovery Process

Like all members of my cohesive team, one key to success when it comes to risk management is the discovery process. Like with other areas of service, when Clay and I meet with clients to discuss their existing risk management structure, we almost always discover significant gaps in protection, opportunities to achieve better results for a lower cost, available income tax savings, or all of the above.

For example, Clay recently went through the discovery process with the CEO of a company in Texas. During the discovery process, he learned that the CEO and his wife owned a large home in Pittsburgh and rented a condo in Texas near the company's offices. The husband traveled back and forth to Texas, but the wife remained in Pittsburgh. In addition, they were in the process of buying another home on a barrier island in Florida with a main house and a guest house.

When Clay reviewed the insurance policies in place, he learned that nothing was coordinated. The CEO and his wife purchased their insurance piecemeal. The result? The couple had a renters' insurance policy they purchased from an agent in Texas and a homeowners' policy they purchased from an agent in Pittsburgh. They also had auto insurance in place with a third agent. They were also in the process of looking for insurance for the Florida home purchase but learned that it was complicated because the island stood at a negative elevation, below sea level. As you might imagine, an island property below sea level is not something many insurance companies insure with off-the-shelf insurance policies. So they were shopping around for a fourth agent to help them figure out what to do to insure the Florida property.

Even more troubling than working with so many different agents was the fact that there was no coordination among them. None of the agents knew the others existed. They didn't know the clients' full financial picture. Each agent was just happy to sell them a policy to cover one sliver of their financial world.

When Clay reviewed the policies, he realized the CEO and his wife could achieve a much better result if they coordinated coverage for all properties and autos, including the new Florida home. As a best-of-the-best independent risk management professional, Clay has access to resources all around the U.S. as well as excess and surplus markets overseas. So he tapped his resources and led a team of agents around the world to replace all of the CEO's piecemeal insurance with a risk management plan that provided better protection and at a lower cost.

While there were many reasons Clay was able to help the CEO and his wife achieve better protection at a lower cost, it all started with the discovery process. The typical professional goes only surface deep when it comes to discovery. The client approaches the agent with an asset they want insured. The agent asks questions about the asset and sometimes a few additional questions. But they don't go beyond the surface level. Oftentimes, they only go surface deep because the agent doesn't have the same network and experience as Clay. So they wouldn't be able to help the client beyond the single asset plus maybe an auto or umbrella policy anyhow. If they revealed the complexity, the potential client would likely keep looking. But as a best-of-the-best independent risk management professional, Clay knows that he can give clients several options to mitigate their risk no matter how complex their world is. And as a member of our cohesive team of experts, he knows he has access to tax, insurance, and other best-of-the-best professionals to coordinate with in case adjustments need to be made outside of the risk management arena to best serve the client.

Thus, Clay is able to go deep with each client to deliver the best risk management solutions available. And it all starts with the discovery process.

Inertia and Unnecessary Exposure to Risk and Liability

When it comes to risk management, lack of coordination and sophistication is just one problem we identify often during the discovery process. Another common problem we encounter is inertia. These successful individuals and families are so busy building businesses and living their lives that they rarely take the time to put together a comprehensive risk management plan or reevaluate insurance plans they have in place. They might intend to but then a year goes by and their life hasn't become any simpler, so they just renew their policies for another year. Even those who do put together a comprehensive risk management plan don't frequently reevaluate them when circumstances change.

"It's amazing the number of times we see an extraordinarily successful individual that could be worth $50, $75, or even $100 million or more have a completely disjointed, uncoordinated risk management portfolio because of inertia," explains Clay. "They build their business, come out of grad school, or get married and put insurance in place, living in a $500,000 home and driving a $35,000 car. Then they build wealth, move into a $4 million home, and drive $100,000 cars and still purchase off-the-shelf insurance policies that are set up for people with dramatically lower risk profiles."

This happens all the time with second or third generation family business owners and even newly wealthy families. "We see a lot of that," says Clay. "They outgrow their current set of risk management advisors but stick with them because that's who they or their parents or grandparents used. Unfortunately, many of the branded risk managers or small independent advisors their parents or grandparents used don't have access to the right tools to efficiently and effectively mitigate their risk."

If you haven't reviewed your risk management plan with a sophisticated, experienced professional like Clay in more than a year, you might be underserved and underprotected without even knowing it. Many successful entrepreneurs and wealthy families are.

The Problem with the Risk Management Industry

While expertise among professionals in many industries varies, the risk management industry is unique in that the advisors need both expertise and access to the right tools to be able to serve successful families well. This is different from many industries where access to tools isn't a barrier. For example, a lawyer who only needs expertise and access to other specialists to defend a lawsuit or put together a complex corporate structure. They don't need tools like a risk manager needs access to sophisticated insurance policies and other tools.

Only a small percentage of risk management professionals have both the best-of-the-best expertise and access to the variety of tools needed to optimize your risk management plan.

"Our industry is a very fragmented industry," explained Clay. "There are a lot of agencies that are very small. They might have 4 to 12 employees. Over the past several years, those agencies have been purchased by other agencies typically backed by private equity money." This consolidation has caused a lot of formerly independent agencies to become small remote offices of larger captive agencies with limited access to tools and expertise as Clay explains below.

The largest number of announced M&A transactions ever in the insurance industry occurred in 2020, beating out the previous high watermark just one year earlier. This activity continued in 2021 and is expected to continue moving forward. This often means fewer options for clients and less independence from the agency side. Years ago, the partners at Simpson McCrady shook hands and committed to not partaking in that consolidation. We felt that being independent and having the size and financial wherewithal to continue to be independent gave us a unique position in the marketplace. For example, we are a very flat organization. We give our producers and our account managers a ton of flexibility in terms of decision-making in accounts that they want to pursue. And we do that because we have the ability to manage ourselves and continue to grow and bring that value to our clients by being independent. A lot of our competitors that have gone through acquisitions have quietly lamented that they can't fulfill the promises they've made to their clients because of a corporate hierarchy and structure. Those structures pull the purse strings and don't allow them to invest where they need to in order to fill the promises they made to their clients.

In the risk management world, sophistication and access to all the tools needed to serve you well is a must in order to be able to receive the right risk management plan and have access to the tools to protect you. That's why we brought Clay and his colleagues at Simpson McCrady onto my core team of specialists. They are committed to serving clients the right way and remaining independent for the foreseeable future. As the industry continues to consolidate, it will make that position even stronger and allow them to continue to deliver on the promises they make to clients.

Optimizing Risk Management within the Structure and Titling of Assets

Because successful private business owners often have assets titled under different corporate names or in their personal capacity, you could inadvertently be underinsured (or not covered at all) for significant losses and not even know it.

"A lot of times the structure, whether assets are held in an LLC, a family limited partnership, other some other structure, is determined by attorneys or CPAs," says Clay. "However, the way attorneys and CPAs have structured assets is often primarily driven by taxes. In these situations, our goal is to make sure that from a titling perspective, protections are in place for our clients and that the policies match to the structure of the existing exposure."

While this concept is often generally understood by professionals in the risk management space, specialists such as Clay know that the inquiry doesn't stop the day the policies are issued. This is especially true when a client is working with the experts who actively monitor changes in tax laws to ensure their clients' assets are always structured in the most tax-favored way. If your legal and tax professionals don't work in lockstep with your risk management professionals, you can end up adjusting how certain assets are titled for tax purposes without realizing you left those assets uninsured by doing so. Unfortunately, this happens frequently when clients coordinate their professionals on their own. And it's one of the most beneficial elements of having a well-coordinated, cohesive team of experts working on your behalf.

But the benefits of risk management don't stop with simply matching insurance to asset titles. Professionals like Clay also help put in place other structures to limit risk based on your actual use of the assets, irrespective of how they are titled. This level of coordination allows business owners and wealthy families to rest assured that their personal and business assets are protected, insured, and tax-optimized at all times.

Hedging Your Bets

Risk management is more than just insuring to replace assets or limit liability. With expert-level service, you can even use risk management strategies to limit the downside of certain high-flying investments while still being able to take advantage of the upside. For example, people I recently spoke to were heavily invested in Bitcoin. In 2020, Bitcoin and other cryptocurrencies shot through the roof. Some people saw their cryptocurrency holdings go from thousands of dollars to millions; others saw their holdings go from millions of dollars to tens or hundreds of millions or even billions of dollars.

While this type of return was certainly not unwelcome, it was not without its downside. If they believed in the future of the investment, they might still believe that the assets had room to run. Even if they did sell, they'd face a significant tax burden by realizing their gains. So they might not want to sell *any* of their investment.

But with such incredible growth, many cryptocurrency investors went from having a relatively small percentage of their net worth to having a huge percentage of their net worth invested in such a speculative and volatile asset. That volatility could have ripple effects on many areas of their lives. Many people who were investing on their own or with professionals who don't understand all risk management options available to investors were selling, unplugging from an investment they believed in, and incurring a significant taxable event.

But what if there were a better way for the investors who wanted to keep their position and lock in gains without incurring a significant tax burden? Without a dedicated professional who understands each client's total financial and family picture, that would not be possible. The client would know what questions to ask, but the professional wouldn't know or have access to tools to help achieve that exact goal. With Bitcoin and other cryptocurrencies, many professionals don't know how to reduce the risk of having an oversized position in something so volatile.

With something as new and exciting as cryptocurrencies, the lack of clarity with most professionals can cause dangerous and unnecessary risk. In this case, it's often risk of inaction. One of the biggest faults with something like cryptocurrencies is that clients are working with professionals who just don't know their options. These professionals don't know there are solutions available to them.

For example, with Bitcoin, many professionals don't know all the ways you can hedge Bitcoin and other cryptocurrency positions. For example, as of this writing, you can create a hedge to lock in a certain value to limit your downside. You can also use opportunity zones to address some of the tax issues. You can even use Bitcoin in a Private Placement Life Insurance policy. There are options available that many people who are working with generalists or unsophisticated professionals are just not familiar with.

Cryptocurrency hedging is another example of the consequences that can happen without any negative intent at all. The advisors really want to do a good job for their clients. They have the right mindset. They have integrity. So it's not like they are intentionally harming their clients. The problem is they don't have all the expertise needed to give their clients the level of sophistication required to optimize their financial world. And many of them don't even know who to ask for help, let alone have their own well-coordinated team of experts at the ready.

To be clear, even I am not an expert at all the areas needed to give the substantive advice and direction we give using the DMMFO model. I have expertise in some areas but not all of them. No one person is an expert in all the areas needed to provide the level of service you deserve. But I know what I don't know and can call anyone in the DMMFO team of core experts to help with issues that arise frequently, or I can call on our extended network of specialists for more nuanced issues that arise infrequently.

That's part of what makes the DMMFO model work so well for our clients. Through me, they have access to the best-of-the-best specialists from around the world without having to worry about finding everyone themselves, coordinating service themselves, being subject to sales pitches every time they take a meeting, or being billed for every phone call to their lawyer or CPA to ask a question. Even more important, they don't have to worry about dealing with people learning on the job. The mistakes people make or opportunities people miss as they learn can cost clients a lot of money. Hedging cryptocurrency investments is just one recent example of how dealing with unsophisticated professionals or people learning on the job (at your expense) can harm the clients these professionals are committed to serving.

 Keys to Chapter

- What the right risk management planning does for your present and your future is like what a home inspector does before you purchase a home. Before you buy a home you intend to live in, you hire an expert to inspect it inside and out, top to bottom, and identify any flaws that need to be addressed.

- On even the smallest homes, inspections often identify dozens of issues that need to be addressed. Sometimes those issues are small. But other times, the inspector finds a crack in the foundation. Until the crack is repaired, the house is in danger. After all, it doesn't matter how beautiful a new kitchen is if the foundation upon which it sits is crumbling.

- When I meet with clients to discuss their existing risk management structure, I almost always discover significant gaps in protection, opportunities to achieve better results for a lower cost, available income tax savings, or all of the above.

- Only a small percentage of risk management professionals have both the best-of-the-best expertise and access to the variety of tools needed to optimize your risk management plan.

- If you haven't reviewed your risk management plan with a sophisticated, experienced professional like Clay Saftner in more than a year, you might be underserved and underprotected without even knowing it. Many successful entrepreneurs and wealthy families are, with substantial personal and real property, inadvertently left unprotected or underprotected.

Chapter 10

Sophisticated Techniques for Simultaneously Managing Risk, Saving Taxes, and Improving Company Profits

As my clients amassed greater levels of wealth, my need for more sophisticated specialists grew. Even small risk management, tax planning, and profit margin improvements can add up to hundreds of thousands or even millions of dollars in benefit to my clients. Over time, that meant I needed to bring even more experienced and sophisticated risk specialists onto my team. And when it comes to captive insurance risk specialists, nobody is better than Wes Sierk.

As the President and Lead Strategist for Risk Management Advisors, Inc., Wes Sierk has more than two and a half decades of experience helping highly profitable, closely held businesses limit their risk exposure and lower their taxes using captive insurance and other sophisticated strategies, including qualified plan structures, onshore and offshore entities, and trust arrangements. He is an internationally recognized expert in the field of captive insurance company design, implementation, management, and risk transfer and has served as an advisor to the United States Congress for issues that affect the financial well-being of young entrepreneurs and their businesses.

Wes is a frequent speaker to industry associations as well as law and CPA firms on asset protection and how ordinary businesses can create their own closely held insurance companies. He has also authored two books: *Taken Captive: The Secret to Capturing Your Piece of America's Multi-Billion Dollar Insurance Industry*, which has become the industry's leading resource for providing basic education and expert guidance on using captive insurance companies in alternative-risk-financing strategies, and *You Can Make It, But Can You Keep It?: A Contrarian Wealth Protection and Risk Management Philosophy*, which discusses the paradigm shift that is necessary for the wealthiest Americans and their advisors when dealing with asset management and protection.

Wes has also been interviewed for or authored many articles in preeminent publications, such as *Builders Exchange Magazine*, the *Journal of Construction Accounting and Taxation*, *Business Insurance*, *The National Underwriter*, the *Los Angeles Times*, *Practical Tax Strategies*, and *California Broker*.

He was awarded the designation of CRIS (Construction Risk and Insurance Specialist) in 2006, and he is one of the few individuals globally to have obtained the Associate in Captive Insurance designation.

How Captive Insurance Specialist and Risk Management Expert Wes Sierk Helps Change the Lives of Clients, Their Families, and Their Businesses

Wes started in the insurance business and was working on nonqualified plans with deferred compensation executive benefits when, in the year 2000, he came across captive insurance companies as an alternative to certain deferred compensation plans. Once he began researching captive insurance as an alternative to deferred compensation plans, he realized captive insurance was not only a good way to accumulate money but also a better way for people to buy their own insurance.

As Wes explains, captive insurance companies are licensed, regulated insurance companies that serve all sizes of businesses. He says easily 80 percent of the Fortune 1000 engage with one or more captive insurance companies, from FedEx and Best Buy to Starbucks and Verizon. BP was able to recoup from the massive oil spill because it had its own captive insurance company and had been putting money away for years to cover a potential environmental disaster. Such well-known companies aside, Wes typically works with industries including manufacturing, construction, home health care, and more. "It's really hard to think of an industry where we don't have one or more clients," says Wes.

In this chapter, Wes shares how he works closely alongside me to use captive insurance as another benefit of working with my DiNuzzo Middle-Market Family Office™.

The Dangers of Captive Insurance When Done Wrong

When considering captive insurance, it's critical to understand that not all captive insurance companies are created equal. People are sold on it being a "Super IRA," but it's not a Super IRA. Insurance companies have tax benefits, but it's a mistake to want to use Captive Insurance only to save taxes. First and foremost, it's a risk management tool that has favorable tax treatment. If your risks are lower than you expect, you can build substantial wealth using captive insurance. But many professionals try to sell captive insurance as a tax dodge, and that's a mistake.

When people buy into captive insurance for the wrong reasons, they buy from someone who just wants to make a sale, or they buy from a captive manager who does not have deep industry and insurance knowledge, it frequently ends up working poorly. As with the other tools my team and I use to help my clients, there are different kinds of captives, each set up in different ways depending on the company and the people running it. When dealing with an unsophisticated professional or someone just looking to sell and move on to the next target, you often end up with a captive that has been set up without getting the type of detail and insight into the company that's needed to put the right plan in place.

I see this during the discovery phase with many clients. With some, I can bring Wes in and fix the plan. But sometimes the plan never should have been recommended to the client at all. For example, in an extreme case, someone sold a captive insurance policy to a dentist in Florida to insure against a snowstorm stopping their business. That's an extreme case, of course, but the point is that, like all the tools in our toolbox, captive insurance is very beneficial for the right person and the right business. But it must be structured properly and used for the right purposes and in the right situations for it to be effective.

In another less extreme case, a business owner in Arizona set up a captive to address some legitimate risks. In this case, the captive manager added a policy to the captive that if the business was audited and the captive was found to be invalid, the captive would pay the penalties, interest, and taxes for the business. That leads to the logical question: if the business owner thought there was a chance the captive wasn't valid, why would they do it in the first place?

Why Forming a Captive Insurance Company Works for Some Private Business Owners

There are two different areas in which Wes sees captive insurance as a solution:

1. Health insurance, workers' compensation, and general liability. "Business owners are looking for a better way to fund their risk long-term," says Wes. "A captive insurance company can be a better, less expensive way for them to cover their risk. Rather than them continually paying, year after year, increasing premiums to the traditional market."

2. When it's hard or impossible for people to find insurance in the traditional market. "A business may be in an industry where they just simply cannot get insurance to cover the risks they have." For example, he works with one of the largest gun-training facilities in the world, which trains special forces, police officers, and SWAT teams. Its workers' comp classification was the same as people who work in traveling circuses.

"It's completely crazy when you look at these trainers, who are highly trained, but they pay the same rate as someone who runs the swing at the carnival. You're overpaying when you pay $1 in a workers' comp premium for every dollar you pay them in wages."

In the traditional marketplace, they were paying $2 million year after year without any real benefits. "Now, in captive, they pay the same $2 million to their own insurance company, but we went out to the global reinsurance market, negotiated, and explained what the gun-training facility did," says Wes. "So they were able to buy reinsurance for about $100,000 which covered any claim more than $500,000, and when the total claims exceed $2 million." They paid the $2 million to their own captive and had absolutely no claims. "Now, instead of being $2 million poorer, they are sitting on $1.9 million in their own captive."

As Wes shows us, captive insurance is a great risk management tool that also provides material tax planning opportunities.

Captive Insurance at Work

In addition to the example above, Wes shares fascinating examples of how captive insurance has been life changing for individuals and companies.

A staffing company that started working with Wes in 2011 (staffing companies represent about 10 percent of his clients because their biggest expense, besides payroll, is workers' comp and health insurance). "We were able to negotiate a really good deal because they do intensive training for their employees, such as forklift training and drug testing," he says. Their workers' comp premium has grown to $17 million a year, but now they have a fully licensed company, and they make more profit from their insurance company than they do from running their staffing business.

Self-storage owners need property insurance, general liability insurance for slips and falls in case somebody gets hurt, and renters' insurance. With captive, says Wes, "they're saving money on insurance, but it's also a profit center because now they're charging an extra $6 to $12 per storage unit," he says. "If you have 150,000 individual doors on your storage facilities, those dollars can add up quickly when you have a 2 percent to 5 percent historic loss ratio."

Opportunities in Captive Insurance

For closely held business owners, captive insurance considerations depend on the type of industry and the number of employees. "A 50-employee company with a young group works great," says Wes, "but 100 employees with an old population doesn't necessarily work—it's a case-by-case basis."

Wes says he's noticed among families working with Multi-Family Offices that they typically buy less insurance than they need because they have plenty of money. The mentality might be: "Oh, well, we don't need to cover this. I can cover it myself. If I get a million-dollar lawsuit, I can pay for it myself."

But high-net-worth individuals are almost always underinsured and are actually losing money with the money-abundant mentality. For example, Wes's office worked with a family that had just wrapped up their operations in China. They had a Falcon 2000 jet they'd paid cash for. When Wes asked to see their plane coverage, they had none, because they figured they could afford to buy another one. The price for a used Falcon 2000 starts at $3.2 million. The insurance cost would have been $40,000 a year. "That's penny-wise and pound-foolish," says Wes.

"The common theme of all my clients is they hate paying insurance premiums," he says. But with captive, "they just hate it a little less when it's their own insurance company."

How to Structure Captive Insurance with the DMMFO

Once you've decided on captive insurance, the next step is working with me and my team, including Wes, to determine which structure works best for your business. "You could get into a deductible program with a traditional carrier where you're taking the first hundred thousand or so, and that will lower your premium," says Wes. "Then there are group captives, which is a bunch of homogenous risk people coming together to take ownership of the risk and share it among themselves."

Wes further breaks it down to frequency risk and severity risk. "For example, if you and I are in a group captive, you would take your frequency risk, meaning the small claims that happen all the time," he says. "But for severity—let's say anything more than $100,000—everyone in the group shares those big ones, so no one really gets hit very hard in the event a member has a catastrophic claim, which will happen in any scenario."

With a group captive, there's no incentive for anyone to overpay. The goal is to pay the least amount of money possible to get out of the traditional market. If you're a group of dentists, a nationwide association sets up a professional liability policy for the dental association, so it's sponsored by the industry and the association. "It's an association captive sponsored by somebody else."

When an individual business sets up a captive with an insurance company to ensure their own risk, they either share some of their risk with traditional reinsurance companies, or they get into a reinsurance treaty with other companies to take half the risk. The other half is spread out among many well-managed captive insurance companies, and each one of them is taking a small share of the risk.

Onshore, Offshore, and Tax Considerations

Captive insurance is not some off-the-wall strategy. As we discussed earlier, the majority of Fortune 1000 companies in the U.S. have at least one captive in place to handle their unique risk management challenges. If done right, it's the same as any other business tool. And we can do it right by partnering with people like Wes who offer customized recommendations on the best domicile for each individual business structure.

About 95 percent of his firm's captive insurance companies are onshore. "You should only be going offshore if there's a specific reason," he says. "If you're a Canadian taxpayer and your business is in Europe, there's no reason to bring that into the U.S. But the majority of U.S. taxpayers should have their captive in the U.S."

Once that decision is made, Wes works with clients to discuss premiums, the most favorable jurisdictions, and tax considerations. Typically, the premiums that captive insurance companies receive and the underwriting profit are *not* taxable as income; the captive pays corporate taxes on realized investment income. Because of this congressionally approved tax treatment for insurance companies, it has been abused by some captive planners and, as a result of this malfeasance, more than 1,500 cases currently sit in tax court.

This is the number one reason for trusting the DMMFO to recruit a reputable firm with experts in this space. Customized solutions keep families out of trouble, and they also provide the comfort level companies need to go about their business. As Wes says, "Would you rather buy a suit off the rack that may or may not fit you, or would you rather go to a tailor and have a bespoke suit made specifically for you and your size, and everything's done perfectly?"

Captive Insurance Risks

"Where I see captives fall apart is when they're not capitalized properly in the beginning," says Wes. "I always recommend people fund a captive the same as you would fund your traditional insurance program for the first couple of years. In the worst-case scenario, you have extra money and reserves, and then you can start dialing back your premiums."

There's a danger in underfunding captives because you want to keep dollars in your business instead of paying your insurance premium. Overfunding is also risky, and Wes mitigates both of these by making sure people are running their captives like an insurance company, with quarterly board meetings and claims reviews. "We organize calls with the clients and make sure everything is documented. Every 't' is crossed and every 'i' is dotted."

"Captive insurance is like poker. It takes five minutes to learn, but a lifetime to master."
—Wes Sierk

Keys to Chapter

- The #1 benefit of captive insurance is that it's a risk management tool. It is a phenomenal risk management tool, and any decisions to implement captive insurance should be based solely on the risk management benefits.
- The #2 benefit of captive insurance is that it's an exceptional tax planning tool.
- When considering captive insurance, it's critical to understand that not all captive insurance is created equal.
- When people buy into captive insurance for the wrong reasons or they buy from an unsophisticated professional or someone who just wants to make a sale, it frequently ends up working poorly.
- The majority of Fortune 1000 companies in the U.S. have at least one captive insurance company in place to handle their unique risk management challenges. If done right, it's the same as any other business tool.

Chapter 11

Significantly Reduce Income Taxes, Improve Cash Flow, and Protect Wealth for Generations

No issues better exemplify the importance of building a cohesive team of experts like wealth transfer, insurance, and business succession. From estate planning to tax strategies to risk management, having the appropriate expert in place to work alongside me in gathering the right input from every expert on my team is critical. That's why I brought international expert Frank Seneco onto my cohesive team of specialists.

For more than 30 years, Frank Seneco has provided advanced planning strategies for a range of ultra-affluent families, businesses, trusts, and individuals so they can grow and protect their wealth for generations.

Frank and his partners at Seneco & Associates, Inc., work with families and individuals who have significant wealth and want to enhance it, tax efficiently transfer it, or protect it from unjust lawsuits, employing many tools to do so, including life insurance, comprehensive retirement planning, sophisticated retirement plans, deferred compensation, and more.

Among other achievements, Frank is recognized internationally as an expert on structuring traditional and Private Placement Life Insurance solutions for entrepreneurs, family offices, and celebrities. In fact, Frank has orchestrated some of the largest Private Placement Life Insurance transactions in the country.

How Wealth Transfer Specialist and Business Succession Expert Frank Seneco Helps Change the Lives of Clients, Their Families, and Their Businesses

Frank does much more than the typical risk management professionals do. For this chapter, I will focus on just two of the ways Frank helps me protect my clients' wealth for their lifetimes and beyond:

1. analyzing existing insurance policies to see how they match my clients' goals, and
2. using sophisticated insurance strategies to make any adjustments needed to reduce income taxes, improve cash flow, and protect wealth for generations.

With respect to analyzing existing policies, Frank and I review everything my clients have in place to see whether the existing insurance policies are the most advantageous in terms of both the big picture and the details. We analyze how the policies tie into everything else my clients have in place. We spot anything missing, such as unintentionally leaving assets uninsured or underinsured. We conduct a complete analysis of what you have in place.

Once we understand your existing policies, Frank and I then analyze opportunities for improvement in your insurance mix. Many clients come to me with dangerous gaps. Others have opportunities for lowering costs or achieving greater efficiencies. If an improvement is available, Frank and I can spot it. And because of the way Frank and I do business, we can provide you with even better, more customized and independent options to improve your insurance portfolio.

When most insurance professionals put together plans, their plans are limited in several respects. For example, many insurance professionals work directly for one insurance company, meaning they can only provide policies from one company. For you, that means it doesn't matter what you need, you're being sold something from the company they represent. Some insurance professionals aren't limited to one insurance company, but they only have access to cookie-cutter policies. It doesn't matter if you have a unique need or need more or different insurance than whatever comes off the shelf. They will tell you you're uninsurable or force you into a policy that doesn't fit your needs.

That's not the case with experts like Frank. Frank's genius comes not just in the strategy but also in his access. He can put together more complicated policies and get you the best underwriting. He can get the best results for you and can ensure you don't overpay. And everything he does puts his clients' interests first. He's not just trying to sell more policies. That's a really key element in all this.

When Frank and I evaluate insurance portfolios as part of the discovery process or during stress testing with new clients, we often discover dangerous gaps in coverage. Their insurance professional may have told the client that they got the "maximum coverage" available (but the truth was it was only the maximum coverage that insurance professional could sell). Or the insurance professional may have told them they were uninsurable (but the truth was they didn't have access to the right underwriting).

Other times we discover that the client had a collection of 18 policies when they really only needed one or two policies. In many of those cases, the 18 policies still didn't protect them adequately (but, again, the insurance professional didn't have the experience, sophistication, network, and *motivation* to help solve the client's actual problem).

To be blunt, there are cases out there where people are oversold insurance—many cases. There are also many cases where the insurance isn't structured right, leaving clients unreasonably exposed. And there are other cases where the policy in place is structured right, but the insurance is not being used effectively.

With insurance, the devil is in the details. The value does not come just from the type of policy or policies in place. The value starts with identifying the right strategy for the client's unique situation. With the right strategy in place, the next step requires choosing the right policy type, the right variables and options within the policy, and having the right carriers and underwriting to pull it all together.

When done right, the client maximizes their benefits for the right price. But very few insurance professionals can put it all together and have access to all the pieces of the puzzle to execute.

Frank does.

For the rest of this chapter, I'll share just some of the ways Frank and I can help you use a sophisticated insurance strategy to reduce income taxes, improve cash flow, and protect wealth for generations.

Auditing and Analyzing Current Life Insurance to Present the Best Options

Years ago, a gentleman who'd started a construction firm approached Frank to buy additional life insurance due to some estate tax issues he anticipated when he passed away. He explained to Frank that he had $4 million of coverage in place that he was sold from another professional and calculated that he needed another $6 million to cover his anticipated tax liability.

When a client comes to me with $4 million in life insurance, they have generally been advised by someone they trust. That's a lot of insurance to purchase from someone you don't trust or without shopping around if the client is buying the insurance themselves. However, in many of these cases, that trust is not justified. Either the professional just wanted to close the sale, earn their commission, and move on, or the professional had good intentions but was operating way over their head when issuing the policies. In this case, it wasn't evident what happened, but the result was just as problematic for the client. "When we reviewed the existing coverage, we found out the policies weren't funded properly," says Frank. "It was also with a company that had been taken over by a larger insurance company, and they weren't funding the policies properly."

Fortunately, Frank was able to spot the problem and restructure the insurance to achieve the needed $10 million benefit for the client. But had the client just gone back to the other professional, who knows what would have happened? He might have been issued policies worth another $6 million and not touched the $4 million policies, leaving him $4 million underfunded because that $4 million of coverage he had in place hadn't been funded properly. And what if the professional made the same mistake with the new $6 million policies? His family could have been devastated upon his death, having to sell the family business and lose their continued income source when the founder passed away, all to pay an estate tax bill that should have been insured against.

This is just one example of why it's so important to reevaluate insurance plans on a regular basis. In this case, Frank's analysis of a new client's existing plan revealed he was dangerously underinsured. But even if Frank and I helped you put the right insurance in place, insurance changes so frequently that you must have an experienced professional reevaluate your existing insurance on a regular basis. For example, because people are living longer, mortality charges and the overall cost of insurance have lowered significantly during the past several years. Many times, you can replace insurance plans when you are 5, 10, or even 15 years older and get the same coverage at a significantly lower cost. Or you can often get additional coverage for the same cost. Additionally, because people's family and business needs change so frequently, the coverage you put in place years ago may no longer be appropriate

"People think they can just set it and forget it," says Frank. "But life's always changing and things are always evolving, so you need to stay on top of this. It's like when a plane takes off from New York and is headed toward Hawaii—you've got your destination, but you have to take into account changes in the weather. A successful business is going to grow, so the focus of the owner is to help increase the value by limiting exposures to risk."

At a minimum, Frank advises reevaluating current insurance every three to five years; this shortens for high-growth companies. A business growing at 20 percent a year needs a hedge in the plan for continued growth, so reevaluating your plans annually or every two years would be appropriate in those cases. Of course, new children or changes in marital status could mean you need different coverage as well.

Sophisticated Defined Benefit Plans

One way to protect wealth for generations and provide significant federal income tax savings is through Sophisticated Defined Benefit Plans, which help achieve a future income benefit to be paid over the participant's lifetime.

"We recently came across a situation with a husband and wife. They were both physicians in their 40s and worked in the same practice," he says. "They had a very small staff and it worked out very well. The gentleman, in particular, was bringing in a tremendous amount of money for the practice."

The couple was living in the tri-state area (New York, New Jersey, and Connecticut) with a very high income tax rate, and his projected income was going to be north of $2.5 million a year for the foreseeable future. As they were living in an area with high income taxes and were in the highest tax bracket, Frank knew that the value of any tax-deferred retirement plans the couple could utilize would be significant

But with their level of income, saving in a traditional 401(k) would not provide much relief. The contribution limits are too low. Fortunately for the couple, the practice had a defined contribution retirement plan in place. However, the defined contribution plan was not set up well enough to help the couple much more than a 401(k) would. The contribution limit was higher, but it was only about $50,000. The couple was only saving about $20,000 or $25,000 in taxes per year from their existing plan.

When Frank looked deeper into the couple's options, he was able to help them put in place a sophisticated defined benefit plan that allowed the couple to make a tax-deductible contribution of $700,000 into a plan that would earn interest and help achieve cash flow for their retirement. It was of tremendous value to find the pretax and tax-deferred growth of the investments for professionals in their 40s. In just that one transaction, they were able to save close to $400,000 in federal income taxes.

"We have to pay our federal income taxes, but we don't have to pay more than required under the regulations. When we have the ability to fund plans like these Sophisticated Defined Benefit Plans and put the money away on your side of the ledger," says Frank, "it makes a lot of sense to do so and not send money to the IRS that you don't have to send them."

Private Placement Life Insurance

Private Placement Life Insurance policies are custom insurance policies that are not available to the general public. They are typically offered outside of the traditional insurance company routes and include both life insurance and variable annuity components. It's a program that's been used by high-net-worth and ultra-high-net-worth families in the U.S. and around the world for decades and can be especially helpful for clients who have significant taxable investment portfolios who want to achieve tax-deferred growth with some degree of liquidity.

Private Placement Life Insurance could be a viable option for somebody who can put money away for a period of time without needing access to the money right away. For the right clients, Private Placement Life Insurance can help save a lot of money in taxes and allow you to pass money to the next generation in a very tax-favored way. For example, private placement policies pay substantial interest rates compared to other saving mechanisms. If structured correctly, you can also pay no taxes on the growth of your portfolio inside the policy. Moreover, many clients like Private Placement Life Insurance because they can have much more say in how the money in the policy is being invested in the first place. Unlike many other policies, you can work with the Investment Advisors that you want and choose investments that fit your profile. You don't just pick from a limited menu of investments.

Additionally, these policies are created in a low-cost structure available only to high-net-worth individuals. Provided they meet certain SEC qualifications, clients can even access their funds easily. Finally, because Private Placement Life Insurance interconnects with estate planning, it's important that any Private Placement Life Insurance efforts are not considered in a vacuum. For the right person, the death benefit associated with the policy can enhance some of the estate-related issues they might have while, at the same time, achieving great investment returns.

"This is not your grandfather's insurance from the local agent," says Frank. "This is a very sophisticated planning tool, and it's very common for people worth $10 million and above."

Premium Financed Life Insurance

When your net worth exceeds or approaches $10 million, a concern some business owners or affluent family leaders have is being able to afford the amount of life insurance they need to save on taxes and protect their assets. Their cash flow doesn't support the premiums they need to pay, especially when they need to invest back in their business to grow it. That has caused many people to become dangerously underinsured. Others have liquidated high-value assets to be able to afford to have the proper insurance in place.

With the right people in your corner, there are multiple ways you can eliminate your risk of being underinsured. One option is to use a tool called Premium Financed Life Insurance, in which you take out loans to pay the premiums for life insurance policies. For many people, taking out loans to afford the right amount of insurance helps avoid much more dangerous or costly outcomes, such as being uninsured or having to sell assets.

"These types of transactions are usually only done by individuals who don't have the ability to completely fund the policy for estate tax purposes, mostly in the estate tax arena," says Frank.

Being able to fund the right amount of insurance for your needs gets extremely complex when your net worth rises and family dynamics become complex. For example, a contractor with five children needed help with his estate plan. He had an exemption amount of roughly $22 million. The accountants and attorneys wanted to use the exemption to move some assets instead of using it toward cash for insurance. When Frank evaluated the proposal, he realized the family didn't have enough gifting ability to achieve their desired outcome. They would still have a $20 million shortfall on their estate tax exposure.

Knowing they lacked the ability to gift the money and also wanting to help the contractor avoid having to pay more than $1 million of premiums, Frank helped the family structure an irrevocable life insurance trust, which would keep the insurance proceeds outside of his taxable estate. Now, the family had $20 million available outside the estate.

Without the expertise of someone like Frank, many successful middle-market business owners end up underinsured, selling family assets to pay the premiums, or having to pay substantial estate taxes upon the parents' deaths. Having someone with Frank's experience on your side ensures you're properly insured and protected both in the present and the future, including significantly increasing cash flow.

Offshore Life Insurance

Offshore Life Insurance works similar to traditional life insurance but, for the right people, can help them save and protect large amounts of wealth.

Although the rules governing Offshore Life Insurance are complex, they can legally shelter significant amounts of money from taxes, including taxes on income from your policy. The rules are incredibly complex, and the vast majority of insurance professionals don't know how to set it up properly, so it's important to be advised by someone like Frank. He and I can help determine whether an Offshore Life Insurance policy is right for you. If it is, we would discuss your options with you and, if you decided to set one up, we would ensure it's put in place legally and legitimately.

While they are not for everyone, they are somewhat common. "We have clients who are Mexican citizens and have changed their tax residency out of the U.S. who have utilized Offshore Life Insurance," says Frank. "Or let's say I have a South American client who wants to get their money out of the U.S. to somewhere like Bermuda. Perhaps they decide they have too much money tied up in U.S. dollars and want to achieve better currency diversification. They could have the ability to take advantage of both tax benefits and currency diversification, plus a number of additional benefits."

Because this is all wrapped in a life insurance policy, certain business owners can achieve all the present benefits of an Offshore Life Insurance policy while simultaneously providing for future generations.

Helping You Make the Best Decisions

When it comes to protecting wealth in the present and for the future, the final piece of the puzzle is to help the client make the best decision.

Like I mentioned earlier, I have multiple ways to achieve goals for our clients. That's why Frank and I work closely with the professionals you currently work with and the rest of my cohesive and well-coordinated team to make sure the insurance recommendations we make fit into the overall plan to help you achieve your goals.

Frank understands exactly how his insurance recommendations fit in succession planning, estate planning, investment planning, tax planning strategies, and countless other parts of your business and life. He knows that his recommendations impact the other areas of the plan and is masterful at understanding what would need to be done by other members of the team with each of his suggestions.

He knows the pros and cons of each recommendation, such as relative income tax savings, liquidity, investment returns, and costs. And he is extremely good at making sure our clients are well aware of all the pros and cons and have the information needed to choose the option they like best. Transparency is essential when you get to this level of client need because unintended consequences can cause substantial negative ripple effects throughout your business and life.

At the end of the day, Frank and I know that my clients have to live with these choices. We do not have to live with them. So we want to make sure you really understand how everything fits together, what everything entails, good and bad, in order to make an informed decision.

Weighing the Pros and Cons

The last point I want to emphasize when it comes to reducing taxes, improving cash flow, and protecting wealth for generations is to beware of the free ride promise. The industry is riddled with salespeople disguised as professionals trying to sell you a defined benefit plan or life insurance policy. Those salespeople come into meetings with you with one objective: to get you to buy the product that pays them the most money. They will say almost anything to close the sale.

The truth is, as with anything my team and I recommend, defined benefit plans and sophisticated life insurance policies come with trade-offs. They can save you a lot of money. They can help you improve and smooth out cash flow. And they can help you protect wealth for generations. But they all have trade-offs. The real value to you comes from understanding the benefits and the trade-offs and then weighing those pros and cons so you can make the best and most informed decision.

Frank does a masterful job of helping my clients understand the advantages and limitations of each option available to them. He also helps them understand how each option fits into the bigger picture of what the rest of my team and I are doing for the client. Then, and only then, is the client able to make the best and most informed decision possible.

Contrast that with how the "salespeople disguised as professionals" operate. Most of the time, they will tell the client only the positive aspects of what they're recommending. They'll often even lie to the client to close the deal, such as telling the client they never have to pay premiums in a Premium Financed Life Insurance policy, that they essentially get free life insurance. Well, that's not even close to being true, and the salespeople either know it and lie or are undereducated and don't know it (and are leading their clients into a disaster).

We help you understand everything you need to know about the options and how they fit into your overall plan. We describe the legal strategy involved in each option. We explain the financial strategy that connects with it as well. And we outline the business strategy, such as corporate benefits, buy-sell agreements, or acting as a funding mechanism for business initiatives. At the end, you will not only be able to make the best decision but you will also understand how every piece of your plan fits together.

Be wary of people who (1) tell you there are no trade-offs with something they recommend, (2) offer a single option, or (3) don't help you understand everything you need to know about the product, why it is a possible good fit for you, and how it fits into your overall goals.

Keys to Chapter

- Sophisticated insurance strategies are some of the many ways my DMMFO can reduce income taxes, improve cash flow, and protect wealth for generations.
- Using sophisticated insurance strategies requires a two-step process.
- First, I work with the best-of-the-best specialists to analyze existing insurance policies to see how they match your goals.
- Second, I present options for any adjustments that could help you save income tax, improve cash flow, and achieve your wealth protection goals.
- Sophisticated Defined Benefit Plans, Private Placement Life Insurance, Premium Financed Life Insurance, and Offshore Life Insurance allow experienced specialists to provide multiple options for reducing income taxes, improving cash flow, and protecting wealth for generations.

Chapter 12

Increase Entity Value and Start Working *On* Your Business, Not Just *In* Your Business

When it comes to my clients' businesses, I understand that even small changes can make big differences in entity value and my clients' lifestyles. I know that if my clients can increase entity value while making their businesses run smoother, they can achieve many other bigger goals. They can decrease financing costs. They can smooth cash flow. They can even spend more time away from the office and with their families. That's why I searched for the best-of-the-best business valuation specialist in the country to bring into my cohesive team. The right business valuation expert not only knows what a company is worth they also understand *why* and what changes a business owner can make to improve entity value. When I searched the country and interviewed experts for possibly bringing onto my team, Melissa A. Bizyak, CPA/ABV/CFF, CVA, stood out as among the best.

Melissa is a partner in the prestigious CPA firm, Grossman Yanak & Ford LLP. She has practiced in public accounting for more than 25 years and concentrates her practice on business valuation and tax-related issues for privately held companies and their owners.

Her business experience is very diverse, including valuations of professional practices, auto dealers, food wholesalers, and equipment manufacturers. She has performed valuations for a variety of purposes, too, including marital dissolutions, buy/sell transactions, dissenting shareholder disputes, and gift and estate tax purposes.

In addition to being a certified public accountant, Melissa is accredited in business valuation and certified in financial forensics by the American Institute of Certified Public Accountants (AICPA). She has also earned the AICPA Certificate of Achievement in business valuation.

Her professional affiliations include the AICPA and the Pennsylvania Institute of Certified Public Accountants, as well as the Estate Planning Council of Pittsburgh. She is also a member of and has served as the Chair of the Executive Advisory Board of the National Association of Certified Valuators and Analysts (NACVA). Melissa has authored numerous articles appearing in professional publications, has written business valuation course-related materials, and serves as a national instructor for NACVA.

When successful middle-market business owners come to me, my discovery process often finds that they are sitting on untapped entity value that can reduce their risks, diversify their income streams, smooth out cash flow, and significantly increase their net worth. However, because they are working so hard in their business and managing their finances, family, and future, these business owners haven't had the time to even pause for a moment to strategize how to increase entity value or what to do with that value as they increase it.

Moreover, just like I mentioned in the beginning of my book, business owners don't know what they don't know. They know their business. They know how to serve their customers. You can't expect them to know all the sophisticated ways to evaluate and increase an entity's value or what tools are available to use that value in a way that doesn't risk the entity. A lot of CPAs and business consultants don't even know how to do that. I do. And Melissa does. She's the expert. That's why I bring her to the table when a client's existing professionals don't have the experience or expertise to help in this important area.

How Business Valuation Expert and Specialist Melissa Bizyak, CPA/ABV/ CFF, CVA, Helps Change the Lives of Clients, Their Families, and Their Businesses

Melissa advises a lot of business owners on strategies to maximize their entity value, reduce risk, and protect their family's wealth. She has a long track record of being able to accomplish those benefits, and more, for clients. And she knows how to work closely with me to help fit her expertise into the bigger picture of what my clients are looking to accomplish. She also works very well with me, other professionals on my team, and any existing experts my clients have in place.

Unlike many CPAs, Melissa doesn't just focus on earnings before interest, taxes, depreciation, and amortization (EBITDA) and spreadsheets. Otherwise, she would not have passed the vetting process to become a core member of my DiNuzzo Middle-Market Family Office™ team of specialists. Instead, she works with me to take the same, relationship-based discovery process with each client. That process reveals not only what each client has in place in terms of business structure and operations but also their goals and risk profiles as well as any specific business or personal needs to which she needs to be sensitive.

When our discovery is complete, Melissa and I present options to the client that we believe could help them achieve their goals. For example, she has a long and excellent track record of helping clients improve cash flow, increase top-line sales, and reduce expenses. Like other core members of the DMMFO cohesive team of specialists, Melissa looks under the hood and suggests only the right tools from her toolbox to present to the client that she believes will address their unique circumstances. Below are some additional ways Melissa helps increase entity values for her and my DMMFO clients.

Litigation Support and Avoidance

One way to increase entity value is through litigation support. Protracted litigation or even the threat of litigation can cost companies a lot of money. Not only that but litigation also distracts the owners and other leaders, which can cause performance to drop, sales to decline, and profits to dwindle. Because businesses generally are valued based on some formula related to sales and earnings, the negative impact of litigation on the company can cause the entity value to drop significantly. Thus, Melissa and I work closely together to help my clients avoid or limit those negative impacts.

"Our practice deals a lot with pending threatened lawsuits for owners of privately held businesses," she says. "When it's in the context of a shareholder dispute, for example, we work on resolving the issue before it goes to court."

In these cases, Melissa works closely with me to approach impending business breakups like a divorce for my clients, acting as a mediator to mitigate the potential financial damage to the business and business owners. "The more people you involve, the more experts you bring in, and the more time you get ready prepping for trial, the more you take away from the end result of what's going in your pocket," she says. "Our job is to get things settled in a way that is advantageous for both sides."

Melissa doesn't just help avoid litigation when disputes arise but she also helps business owners create exit planning strategies while the business is operating smoothly as an additional way to avoid sticky situations in the future. Working closely with me and other professionals, as necessary, Melissa comes to the table with practical considerations and solutions. "We'll go in and present on potential triggering events, and how it speaks to value," says Melissa.

Valuation Gaps and Opportunities

The other side of Melissa's business is how she works with me to conduct valuations for other purposes, such as financial reporting, equitable distributions by transactions, dissenting shareholder disputes, employee stock ownership plans, or ESOPs, and gift and estate tax purposes. "Highly specialized valuation is more than just accounting and finance," she says, referring to the behavioral issues and family dynamics that require special care. There's a good bit of art as well as science in what she does.

"Our sweet spot is privately held businesses," says Melissa. "My typical client is anywhere between $5 and $10 million, or up to $100 million in manufacturing, services, engineering architects, and distribution whole-sale markets." She's in the classic space of successful, multigenerational, privately held, closely held companies in need of valuation expertise.

Learning the family dynamics is the first step in my discovery process. "We need to understand the thoughts, the wishes, the goals," says Melissa. "We're there to really customize and advise and help find out what is pos-sible, what is achievable."

The most common scenario Melissa and I encounter is business own-ers not planning well ahead of time. "So we need a sufficient runway to bridge the gap between where the business is and where we need it to be to fulfill the objectives of the business owner." It's always amazing how com-panies worth many millions or a billion-plus, especially privately held, closely held businesses, fail to plan ahead. It's understandable, however, when we remember how thin these business owners are stretched.

Increasing Cash Flow and Decreasing Risk

Two of the most common goals successful middle-market business owners have are to increase cash flow for the business and decrease busi-ness and personal risk. Like any member of my cohesive team, Melissa works to identify several ways to achieve both of those goals.

For example, she helps evaluate the following questions with the busi-ness leaders.

- How can we increase topline revenue or sales?
- How can we generate more revenue from customers, clients, or the people with whom we do business?
- Can we break into new markets?
- Can we diversify product-wise?

"Oftentimes when we get into privately held businesses, the owners and their advisors are very focused on minimizing taxes," says Melissa. "That's a great thing but, at the same time, that really flies in the face of maximizing value when you're only focused on tax minimization." Melissa takes a different approach, working simultaneously on tax minimization as well as reducing business expenses, increasing revenue, improving profit margins, and many other ways to add total value to the entity.

"How can we improve margins?" she will ask. "If we increase the top line and we're buying in greater volumes, then we'll likely have higher gross profit margins because we have greater buying power." She'll then explore options for achieving that goal with me, other members of my cohesive team, and the leadership of the company.

For example, if your company has been stockpiling cash for a rainy day, putting money under a mattress, and you don't have debt, you likely have excess working capital that the DMMFO and its partners can help put to work to provide greater returns to your equity holders. You could also be running at negative working capital. "And we'd work with you to solve that," says Melissa. Managing working capital means asking such questions as

- How do you manage your payables?
- Are you leveraging your payables?
- Are you collecting your receivables, and in a timely manner?
- Are you turning over inventory in line with the industry?

"We're able to make a big difference and impact when we bring in ideas," says Melissa, "because what they realized typically at the outset, engaging someone like me or my team, is that we do nothing but this full time." She also has the benefit of having looked under the hood at hundreds, if not thousands, of companies all around the country. She's seen what works and what doesn't work. She learns from multiple industries. She knows what to look for and what options are available to resolve even the most complex challenges.

What are some of the misconceptions about business valuation Melissa runs across? "One of the biggest stumbling blocks we have is just what's been filled in the business owners' heads," she says. "Business brokers call.

They want you to work with them. They want to sell your business, and they're going to promise you the world."

Instead, Melissa only promises a genuine relationship and professional, sophisticated approach to help you maximize your entity value for whatever goals you have. As she says, "We're there to serve the client in the best way that we can. They decide what that means, and we help them achieve it."

Keys to Chapter

- When successful middle-market business owners come to me, my discovery process often finds that they are sitting on untapped entity value that can reduce their risks, diversify their income streams, smooth out cash flow, and significantly increase their net worth.

- However, because they are working so hard, many business owners haven't had the time to pause for a moment to strategize how to increase entity value or what to do with that value as they increase it.

- Increasing entity value involves more than just EBITDA and spreadsheets. It involves the same relationship-based discovery process to understand what's currently in place, the client's goals, and what options are available to the business owner.

- Increasing entity value also involves risk management, litigation support and avoidance, understanding family dynamics, and business operations optimization.

- My cohesive team and I, including business valuation expert Melissa Bizyak, can work closely with any professionals you have in place to understand and provide you with options that many business valuation experts either don't consider or don't have the experience and expertise to identify.

Chapter 13

Access Alternative Investment Solutions

Peter Sasaki, MBA, began his career in 1991, as Vice President and Proprietary Trader of foreign currencies, fixed income securities, equity securities, and commodities at J.P. Morgan, where he spent the first six years of his career after earning a BA in philosophy from Pomona College and an MBA in finance from the Stern School of Business at New York University.

After leaving J.P. Morgan and spending three years at Moore Capital, Peter founded Logos Capital Management, a global macro hedge fund. Today, Peter is a managing member of private investment firm CGS Associates, and he helps high-net-worth clients access traditional and alternative investment solutions in a number of capacities, most notably as cofounder of SDS Family Office, an entity that combines a number of Single Family Offices for ultra-wealthy families, as well as a member of my core DiNuzzo Middle-Market Family Office cohesive team of specialists. He also serves as a trustee of Pomona College and Hopkins School.

Peter provides a broad range of expertise to family members with a portfolio focus on difficult-to-access, best-in-class investments in private equity, venture capital, and marketable alternatives. He has expertise in family offices, endowment and foundation management, portfolio construction, and asset allocation, and cowrote the book *Maximizing Your Single-Family Office Leveraging The Power Of Outsourcing And Stress Testing* with Russ Alan Prince. He also has a deep background in marketable hedge fund strategies, including global macro, commodities, fixed income, equities, and emerging markets, as well as less liquid alternative investments, including agriculture, real estate, private equity, and venture capital.

How Family Office Expert and Investment Specialist Peter Sasaki Changes the Lives of Clients, Their Families, and Their Businesses

Peter and I work closely together to help clients access a full range of investment options while reducing risk, diversifying exposure to asset classes, and achieving optimal returns within their investment risk profiles. His specialty involves accessing alternative investment options, including hedge funds, private equity, and venture capital investments.

In addition to his investment knowledge, Peter's clients structure their investments within the alternative investment world to reduce risk and maximize liquidity—two outcomes many Investment Advisors don't know how to achieve. He does so in part by using principles he has mastered through participation in the management of large education endowments as well as various family foundations, which I discuss in more detail below.

Moreover, Peter also offers my clients unprecedented access to a wide variety of alternative investments due to his extensive network of hedge fund, private equity, and venture capital executives. This means he can help clients choose between many more options within each alternative asset class.

Peter's depth of knowledge of the alternative investment world and access to options within that world are second to none.

The Human Element and Personal Touch

Having Peter on my team doesn't just help my clients access more and better alternative investments. Peter and the rest of my core team members understand that their work doesn't happen in a vacuum. Their work is performed in the context of what the other professionals are doing for my clients. And that requires a different level of coordination, skill, and sophistication, which most professionals are unable or unwilling to provide. After all, as I frequently discuss with my DMMFO clients, what good is growing your wealth if you're unhealthy or unhappy? Whatever I do needs to be conducted as part of a plan that allows you to achieve goals far beyond your financial wealth. As I mentioned above, everything I do is designed to allow you to spend more quality time with your loved ones and improve your physical and mental wellness, including when it comes to growing your investments. With virtually unlimited investment options, there's no reason to recommend ones that add stress to your life or take time away from your business or family life.

One of the first steps to being able to recommend the right alternative investments to my clients is understanding the human element to investing. "You have to understand people's temperaments to adequately serve your clients. I have one client who is a venture capital manager. He told me that I'm supposed to run everything. So I set up his accounts and served him like I do all my clients. As I checked on his portfolio, however, I noticed he had been trading securities on his own. If something was doing really well, he'd sell it. If something wasn't doing well, he'd sell it. After talking with him, I realized he didn't want an advisor. He wanted an investment coach. So, from that point forward, I became his investment coach, and it's working out very well."

This level of understanding extends beyond simply appreciating their risk tolerance or how much control they want to maintain. We need to understand how the investments fit within the big picture of their life. "Let's say the client is an entrepreneur who owns 10 percent of their company. They want out and are starting to do some planning. They call you up and say, 'P. J., I'm thinking of selling half my stake in the company.' You gather me and a few other specialists on the team to talk through their options. As we learn more from the client, we might realize they are mentally carrying the value of their shares at a completely different value than what someone would be willing to pay for it. As you know, this disconnect requires us to dig deeper into the client's true motivations for considering selling half their stake because we might be able to help them achieve the same result without having to sell. Or, one of the team specialists, such as Melissa, might be able to help them implement a few changes that could increase their entity value."

Peter's thought process represents exactly why the DMMFO model is so valuable. He recognizes that what might start out as a question involving how to invest the proceeds of a company sale might end up with the company not being sold at all. He knows we need to understand the client's real goal so we can help identify options for achieving them, even if that means he isn't involved in the solution. And he's sophisticated and experienced enough to be able to identify when there's a disconnect between what the client called about and what the client actually needs.

"You become a counselor in many matters like these when a client calls saying they are thinking of one solution and you learn that they really need another solution," Peter observes. "This is something lawyers do quite frequently for ultra-wealthy clients that is rarely available to middle-market business owners. I've had these conversations with an entrepreneur looking to sell their company. I work with either an investment bank or a family office, preparing to find the best bid or the best exit strategy. And then, as I learn the client's true goals, we end up realizing the client might be better served holding onto the company for one reason or another, while still being able to achieve their big-picture goal another way."

Another scenario that comes up often involves a business owner who is uncomfortable having so much of their net worth tied up in their company. They continue to invest in their company because they need to, but they've tied up 100 percent of their family's future into that one investment. Although they have more knowledge, experience, and control over this one company, they realize having all their eggs in one basket is risky.

In these cases, I might help the client create liquidity and then work with Peter and others on my team to diversify their investments for better security.

After completing my discovery process and gaining an understanding of the human element for each client, Peter and I begin to consider whether alternative investments might be a useful option for each client. While alternative investments encompass a wide variety of strategies, the most common ones include hedge funds, private equity, and venture capital investing. Other investments include special purpose acquisition companies, or SPACs, small business syndications, or even investment banking financing options.

"There are tremendous opportunities in the alternative investment world if you know what you are doing," says Peter. "But you need to do your homework to understand exactly what you are investing in and who the key players are with respect to getting a return on your investment. For example, somebody I know recently sent me the PowerPoint deck regarding an opportunity to own real estate that's leased to a large franchise. On the surface, the numbers looked good; however, you must understand when investing in something like this that your return on investment depends on the people involved in operating the business. You're investing in them. You need to have enough information about them to evaluate whether the investment is a smart one." With that investment opportunity, Peter recommended against investing in that business.

Getting into *the Right* Hedge Funds, Private Equity, or Venture Capital

As with everything we recommend, investing in hedge funds, private equity, or venture capital is not without its trade-offs. Choosing which funds to trust with your money is not as simple as in the Mutual Fund world, warns Peter. "With hedge funds, along with private equity and venture capital investing, it's really important to acknowledge that, in addition to any fees, pedigree and brand name really matters. I would only want to be invested in groups that are in the top quartile. There is such a difference, particularly in private equity and venture capital, between top decile funds and everybody else and top quartile funds and everybody else."

In the Mutual Fund world, Peter explains, "if you end up investing in an average fund and the market goes up, you're still generally fine. Maybe you leave a percent on the table, which over time isn't going to add up to a lot. But you can really get hurt if you invest in a hedge fund, private equity, or venture capital fund that isn't a top performer."

This creates a big problem in the world of hedge funds, private equity, and venture capital. Simply put, a lot of people can help you get into those investments but only a small percentage of Wealth Managers can get you into *the right* hedge funds, private equity, and venture capital funds. "There's such a performance difference across these types of investments. That's why I don't tell people 'I'm going to buy a macro hedge fund tomorrow.' First, I would never buy one; I'd spread out the investment across several. Second, I would identify around five that I know to be high quality and invest in those specific funds."

Finally, Peter notes how important the people behind the funds are to whether he would consider proposing one to a client. "From a top down macro point of view, this business is still about trust more than anything else. I want to be dealing with people that have excellent reputations. Because these classes of investments are less regulated, they require much more due diligence than traditional ones. We need to know who is in charge of any fund we consider before we would recommend it to a client. We need to know who we are dealing with when any of our clients invest in a fund. We need to really understand everyone involved in coordinating and running that investment. This information helps us understand their mentality, where they're coming from, and where their interests might diverge from yours."

Investment Banking Options

Investment banking involves buying, selling, or financing businesses. "We have access to a wide variety of investment banking driven options through the DiNuzzo Middle-Market Family Office," says Peter. "From debt offerings to leveraged asset purchases to cash deals, we have a number of opportunities available to middle-market business owners if they want to diversify into other privately held businesses."

With investment banking, having the right specialists on your side is very important. Otherwise, you could end up with your money tied up in a bad investment for years. Like private equity and venture capital options, it's important to know the people involved and all costs that are relevant to your investment. "Does the person who found the deal want to get paid a fee for putting the deal together? That's one question to ask," says Peter. "Another is, 'Do you know enough people that you're able to do this without risking too much of your own money?' People with less than $25 million to invest are typically still working on building their business. They don't know other people to co-invest with, so they might need help from their advisor's network to raise enough money for certain deals that everyone can get in without overextending themselves."

"I'm currently working on a deal with a family that is putting up the first $5 million," says Peter. "They need another $45 million to complete the deal. That deal is going to close with an investment bank that is going to charge a fair bit to the whole group. But the original sponsor, the person who found the deal, is getting the terms that they want. The investment banker found other family offices and small institutions that aren't competitors."

Only a fraction of 1 percent in the investment world have the access and capabilities to put together deals of that magnitude in a way that works out for all parties involved. Peter is one of the few who can both access the right alternative investments and get deals closed.

Helping You Use an Endowment Model to Invest in Alternative Investments

While not suitable for everyone, an endowment model may be advisable for certain investors, as the model has historically generated stronger returns with lower risk through various economic and investment climate cycles than traditional domestic stock and bond portfolios. The people who achieve the best returns with the addition of private equity, venture capital, and alternative hedge strategies use this portfolio model and invest in a variety of funds to take advantage of the potential for outsized returns while maintaining some liquidity over time. This is similar to the approach of the most successful endowments, pensions, and foundations including the private family foundations and educational institutions—Pomona College and Hopkins School—that Peter serves.

When you work your way up the Private Wealth Hierarchy to experienced Wealth Managers, you might start to hear about investing in private funds. Unfortunately, what you don't hear from most Wealth Managers is that not all venture capital, private equity, or hedge funds are created equal. Some offer little or no advantages to traditional investments. Additionally, even the great ones have good years and bad years. Finally, they often have long lockup periods that make the investments illiquid for a number of years.

As Peter notes, "Private equity's an interesting way of buying equities. It correlates with public equities, but it often delivers higher returns and is less volatile. So it can be an important part of your portfolio." But private equity, like venture capital, often requires larger minimums and long holding periods, so the trade-off is liquidity. When you have tremendous funds like the ultra-wealthy families, endowments, or pensions, that's not much of an issue. They can sign up for one private equity fund with a seven-year payout, another one year later, and so forth. "Endowments and pension funds can easily create rolling vintages of maturity dates, which is important because, like all products or asset classes, private equity has good investments and bad investments, good years and bad years. The worst thing you can do is have all your money tied up in one bad fund for seven years or longer."

With less than $25 million to invest, you can still access similar returns in private equity by "finding a way to be able to replicate what we call vintages in the fund business and have that exposure over the years," Peter says. "To really do it like an endowment, you'd want, at a minimum, between $5 million and $25 million, with the lower-end investing more in newer solutions becoming available, such as high-quality funds of funds. In these cases, you need to be very careful to understand any fees involved to make sure the returns justify the fees because sometimes they don't. I hesitate to pay fees to Mutual Funds because they all generally correlate with and look like the stock market. However, once we get into private equity, venture capital, and other private asset classes, I'm willing to pay fees as long as the returns are there."

Keys to Chapter

- One of the first steps to being able to recommend the right alternative investments to our client is to understand the human element to investing. This level of understanding extends beyond simply appreciating their risk tolerance or how much control they want to maintain. I need to understand how the investments fit within the big picture of their life.

- Many business owners grow uncomfortable having so much of their net worth tied up in their company. They continue to invest in their company because they need to, but they've tied up 100 percent of their family's future into that one investment.

- While alternative investments encompass a wide variety of strategies, the most common ones include hedge funds, private equity, and venture capital investing. Other investments include special purpose acquisition companies, or SPACs, small business syndications, or even investment banking financing options.

- As with everything we recommend, investing in hedge funds, private equity, or venture capital is not without its trade-offs. There are also big differences, particularly in private equity and venture capital, between the top funds and everybody else. That's why working with experts who have access to the top funds is so important. The same is true with SPACs, small business syndications, and investment banking options.

- With so many options available to successful middle-market business owners, finding the right option for you remains critical. In addition, how you structure your investment can make an impact on both risk and return on your investment. Some investors could see increased results using an endowment model like the ones used by family foundations and educational institutions.

Chapter 14

Succession, Exit, and Estate Planning

Bradley (Brad) J. Franc, Director, is an attorney and former certified public accountant at an international CPA firm. He has been practicing law for more than 30 years, now working as a director in the Business Law and Estates and Trust Groups at the prestigious Pittsburgh law firm, Houston Harbaugh, P.C., and has earned several prominent recognitions in the legal community including being named an AV Preeminent® rated attorney by Martindale-Hubbell's Peer Review Rating system, being selected to the Pennsylvania Super Lawyers list, attaining a Five Star recognition as a Wealth Manager, estate planning attorney, and financial services professional, and more.

Today, Brad focuses his practice on helping private business owners, affluent individuals, and closely held businesses, strategically integrate their business, estate, and charitable planning objectives. He works closely with each client on strategic planning, commercial transactions, corporate governance, and estate and succession planning. For example, Brad has helped form, acquire, and sell many manufacturing, high-tech, and service-related companies. He's raised capital through private placements. He's negotiated and secured financing from both traditional and alternative capital sources. And he's structured sophisticated estate and succession plans to help closely held business owners and high-net-worth individuals all over the country.

In addition to his professional work, Brad is a successful entrepreneur. Brad has started and exited three separate companies and made the Inc. 5000 fastest-growing companies list nine times in a 20-year period. Recently, he formed The Succession Coach LLC to provide succession and strategic planning to closely held business owners.

A frequent lecturer and author on closely held business and tax topics, federal and state tax issues, and estate planning, Brad has written many useful articles, including an article about tax provisions that has even been cited by the Supreme Court of the United States. He has appeared on Bloomberg Television and Fox News websites for his business, tax, and succession planning advice and has been published in U.S. News & World Report.

Brad also created The Succession Solution^{SM}, a customized program to assist closely held businesses in their transition to the next generation. The Succession Solution^{SM} is a customized process that builds a realistic and practical framework for the transfer of business and wealth. It addresses the risks and dangers the business and the owner may face while fully utilizing the owner's leadership values, wisdom, and responsibility. He documented that program in his best-selling book by the same name, *The Succession Solution: The Strategic Guide to Business Transition*.

How Succession Planning Expert and Specialist Brad Franc, Esq., Helps Improve the Lives of Clients, Their Families, and Their Businesses

When it comes to the impact the DiNuzzo Middle-Market Family Office™ makes on our clients' lives, succession, exit, and estate planning are among the most impactful. That's because the difference between an expert succession, exit, and estate plan and one created by a less experienced professional (or having no plan) can be huge. With the wrong (or no) succession, exit, or estate plan, families can be left losing control of family businesses, having to sell precious family assets, or paying hundreds of thousands or even millions of dollars in unnecessary taxes.

Brad helps me put together sophisticated succession, exit, and estate plans to help clients optimize their business value and achieve maximum control over their businesses and family wealth in the present and the future.

With respect to succession and exit planning, Brad uses a proven process he created called The Succession Solution^SM to help create and implement a succession plan for my clients that helps them achieve bigger business, financial, family, and philanthropic goals. I'll walk you through the big picture of how The Succession Solution^SM works.

Next, I'll discuss how Brad helps clients navigate the ever-changing business, legal, and tax regulations with estate planning to minimize taxes, maximize control, and protect assets from outside interests.

The Succession and Exit Planning Problem

According to PwC's Global Family Business Survey 2021, only 30 percent of family businesses have any formalized succession plan, which is up from just 15 percent in 2018.[1]

Why does this matter? According to the Family Business Institute, only about 30 percent of family-owned businesses survive into the second generation, with only 12 percent still viable into the third generation, and about 3 percent operating into the fourth generation and beyond.[2]

These two sets of statistics paint a bleak picture for closely held family businesses, and it's likely no coincidence that the percentage of businesses with formalized succession plans closely resembles the percentage of businesses that survive to even the second generation. If the survival statistics are that grim, why don't more closely held business owners put a plan in place?

---

1   PwC, Global Family Business Survey 2021: From Trust to Impact: Why Family Businesses Need to Act Now to Ensure Their Legacy Tomorrow, PwC, 2021, https://www.pwc.com/gx/en/family-business-services/family-business-survey-2021/pwc-family-business-survey-2021.pdf.

2   Family Business Institute, Family Business in Transition: Data and Analysis, Part 1 (of 3), 2016, https://www.familybusinessinstitute.com/wp-content/uploads/2019/01/Family-Business-Succession-Planning-White-Paper.pdf.

In his book *The Succession Solution*^{SM}, Brad describes several reasons, including the following:

- Conflicts in the family business
- Fear of the unknown
- Advisors overcomplicating the process
- Too many advisors saying too many different things
- Self-serving advisors
- Lack of potential successors
- Confusing succession planning with estate planning
- Cultural differences or tensions between generations
- Fear of having their weaknesses exposed
- Fear of success and being pushed out sooner than they want

While these reasons are valid, there's nobody I trust more to help my clients create their best outcome and work through all of those concerns, and more, than Brad. You didn't survive in business this long by shying away from tough challenges. And with the experience, expertise, and systemized approach that Brad can bring to you and your business, you can do the same with succession planning. In addition, Brad can guide you and all relevant stakeholders through the challenging conversations in a way that positively impacts you and your family for generations.

The Succession Solution^{SM}

Brad sees succession planning for closely held businesses as the (1) development, (2) execution, and (3) subsequent review and adjustment of a plan to transfer your business or position in the company to the next generation of managers or owners. Importantly, the next generation is not *always* family. As you'll learn, for some families, the business is best left in the hands of hired professionals, employees, or an unrelated third party. Other times, some or all family members want to remain in the business in some capacity.

To help closely held business owners identify and execute the best plan for their situation, Brad developed The Succession Solution^{SM}, a unique step-by-step process that guides business owners through clearly defined stages before taking specific actions or making final decisions. When he takes business owners through each of the defined stages, the likelihood of success increases dramatically. Moreover, by following a defined and proven process, business owners, employees, family members, and all other stakeholders gain clarity and confidence that they have addressed the most important issues. And that increases the likelihood that everyone will support, adopt, and help implement the plan.

The Foundation to The Succession Solution^{SM}

For a complete description of each step of The Succession Solution^{SM}, I highly recommend reading Brad's book. However, with his permission, I'll be sharing the high-level points and foundation in this chapter to demonstrate how Brad expertly helps my clients using The Succession Solution^{SM}.

At its core, The Succession Solution^{SM} works by addressing the four fundamental communities within a company from the start: ownership, governance, leadership, and employment. These four communities matter most to the company's continued viability, and each needs to have clear policies, procedures, and rules in place so everyone in the company is on the same page with respect to roles and responsibilities. This benefits the company both in the present and the future.

In addition, The Succession Solution^{SM} follows the premise that "fair may be equal but equal may not be fair." There are key differences between equal and fair and even different levels and lenses of fairness within an organization. For a simple example, assume a father started a business 30 years ago. His wife has since passed away, and he wants to pass along the business to his two daughters. The "equal" way to do that would be to pass 50 percent of his ownership and 50 percent of management to each daughter. But what if one daughter has no interest in running the business? What if one daughter isn't wired to make good management decisions or has a drug problem? What if the daughters don't get along?

In any of those situations, it might not be "fair" to transition equal ownership and management to each daughter. It wouldn't be fair to force management responsibilities on the daughter who has no interest in running the business. It wouldn't be fair to the business, employees, or the daughter if the owner transfers management responsibilities to the daughter who isn't wired to make good decisions or who has a drug problem. And it wouldn't be fair to anyone to leave 50/50 management to two people who don't get along.

By guiding all relevant stakeholders through The Succession Solution℠, Brad helps focus on achieving the *right* succession or exit plan for the family and all four fundamental communities in the company.

The Succession Solution℠ also helps get everyone on board by providing a *fair process*, rather than promising even a *fair outcome*. Brad has found that we can't always predict or ensure a particular outcome (who would have predicted the COVID-19 pandemic and its impact). As a result, it is more important to ensure a fair process. A fair process ensures that all relevant stakeholders are heard, acknowledged, and valued but doesn't promise that all relevant stakeholders are going to love the results. In the example above, the daughter with a drug problem might not believe it is fair to cut her out of a management role and give her company shares through a trust. But that might be the decision made by the owner by following The Succession Solution℠ process, a proven, fair, step-by-step process to set up, execute, and update a succession plan.

Once these fundamentals are understood, the stakeholders are ready to follow six stages to set up, execute, evaluate, and update a successful plan. I'll briefly introduce each of these steps below.

The Purpose Stage

Brad believes that the initial stage of any succession plan is establishing your purpose. Your purpose lays the foundation for the entire project.

In *The Succession Solution℠*, Brad shares a verse from the Bible that states, "Where there is no vision, the people perish." The Purpose Stage of

The Succession Solution[SM] helps you set that vision for your company and all important stakeholders.

Understanding your purpose helps you develop an effective plan in several ways. For example, it helps you filter decisions to determine which would help you better achieve your desired purpose. It also helps you get key stakeholders to understand and buy into the process. It shows you what success looks like.

In addition to defining your purpose and understanding what success looks like, Brad helps people define what *failure* looks like in the Purpose Stage. Understanding what failure looks like also helps you filter decisions to determine whether one option would lead you closer to failure than success. Additionally, understanding what failure looks like can be a great motivator. Often, business owners are more motivated by avoiding failure than achieving success.

Once you complete the Purpose Stage, you will have established your fundamental principles, vision, and reason for developing your succession plan. You will also understand what success and failure look like for you, your family, your company, and other relevant stakeholders. Together, this information will make the rest of the succession planning process much easier and more effective.

The Discovery Stage

As Brad notes in his book, "You first need to determine where you are before you can get to where you want to be." That's where the Discovery Stage comes into play.

"When you walk into a shopping mall and need to find the Apple store, what do you do first?" Brad asks. "If you're like me, the first thing you do is look for the big block structure with a map of the mall. When I find the map, I immediately look for the red dot that says, 'you are here.' Then I can figure out how to get to the Apple store. The Discovery Stage is the 'red dot' of succession planning."

The Discovery Stage begins by taking an inventory of the existing structure of your business, family, and ownership including, for example, reviewing the following items, and more:

- Form of business—corporation, LLC, partnership.
- If it's a corporation, is it an S-Corp or a C-Corp?
- Who are the owners and how much do they own?
- Are there shareholder agreements in place? If so, how do they impact your plan?
- Who are the members of your board of directors?
- Who are the officers?
- Who are the key employees?
- Do you have employment agreements with key employees?
- Family dynamics: do you have family members inside the business?
- Financial condition or net worth of the business owner.
- Obligations to banks and other third parties.
- Important customer and supplier relationships.
- Key assets outside of the business, such as real estate, for example.
- What succession planning is already in place?

As Brad explains, "During the Discovery Stage, you will likely discover issues you did not fully understand or had forgotten. Identifying them at this stage will allow you to better plan for succession."

At the end of the Discovery Stage, you will understand exactly what your red dot looks like. That, combined with the purpose and goals you set during the Purpose Stage, empowers you with both the red dot and the destination. Over the rest of The Succession Solution℠ process, you will connect the dots between where you are today and where you and your company want to go.

The Challenge Stage

"Completing the Challenge Stage of The Succession Solution℠ solidifies the foundation of your successful plan" explains Brad. "During the

Challenge Stage, we identify potential threats to your plan so you reduce your risk of being blindsided or sacrificing precious time needed to transform or overcome those threats."

In essence, the Challenge Stage follows a slightly modified SWOT analysis process. Through the traditional SWOT analysis process, you identify Strengths, Weaknesses, Opportunities, and Threats. In the context of succession planning, however, threats and weaknesses are often the same, so the Challenge Stage of The Succession Solution℠ combines those into one analysis, which Brad refers to as simply Obstacles.

Thus, during the Challenge Stage, Brad works with you to identify your Strengths, Opportunities, and Obstacles. Generally speaking, for our purposes, here's what each of those terms means in the context of The Succession Solution℠:

- Strengths refer to your company's ability to accomplish tasks.
- Opportunities refer to matters you and your team are excited about, such as developing new skills, generating company-wide optimism for the future, or increasing customer security. (Opportunities are often the results that will occur by resolving or overcoming your obstacles.)
- Obstacles are the threats or potential dangers blocking you from achieving your ideal succession, such as family discord, an unprepared successor, refusal to cede control, potential tax obligations, or losing a key employee.

With these listed, Brad then works with you to identify which of those obstacles are controllable so you can start planning how to mitigate or overcome them as you put your plan together, which happens next, in the Mission Stage of The Succession Solution℠.

The Mission Stage

The Mission Stage is where the rubber hits the road and you establish goals, action steps, and key performance indicators to help you track performance. But before you start moving, you need to put together a plan.

That's why the first step of the Mission Stage of The Succession Solution^{SM} is goal setting.

"Establishing goals is central to the Mission Stage, and I am a firm believer in the SMART approach when it comes to setting goals," Brad explains, adding that he uses SMART as "an acronym for Specific, Measurable, Agreed, Realistic, and Timely. When it comes to succession planning, setting realistic, timely, and measurable goals that all relevant stakeholders understand and agree with is critical to success."

Brad recommends setting long-term goals and then breaking them down into one-year goals as well as quarterly goals, with each time frame building up to the other. Your quarterly goals should lead you closer to your annual goals, which should lead you closer to your long-term goals.

In the next stage of The Succession Solution^{SM}, Brad helps you break down your goals into manageable chunks and get started on executing your plan.

The Annual Review Stage

At this point in The Succession Solution^{SM} process, you have a big-picture plan in place for your business. But this is where many business owners go wrong. Indeed, this is where even some of the more skilled professionals go wrong. They create a succession plan, but it falls apart because it is too big or complex to implement. The business owner doesn't know what they need to do next.

Brad and The Succession Solution^{SM} help avoid this outcome using the Annual Review Stage and the Quarterly Review. After completing the Mission Stage, Brad helps you decide which goals you want to accomplish over the following year.

As with your longer-term goals, Brad uses the SMART approach to set goals that are Specific, Measurable, Agreed, Realistic, and Timely for one-year goals. Then, he helps you identify obstacles and specific actions that must be completed to achieve your one-year goals, making sure everyone leaves the meeting with clarity on the following:

- Your Annual Goals

- Obstacles to Achieving Your Annual Goals
- Action Steps Needed to Achieve Your Annual Goal
- Key Performance Indicators to Measure Success

When working through the Annual Review Stage, Brad helps you prioritize your goals by importance and break down the big steps you need to achieve into more manageable chunks. In the next stage, Brad helps you put quarterly action steps together to help you execute.

The Quarterly Review Stage

"There's a great book called *The 12 Week Year*, by Brian Moran," Brad says. "In it, Moran takes the position that people can achieve the equivalent of a year's worth of productivity in a 12-week time frame with a plan and focused action. By setting quarterly and annual goals, in addition to longer-term goals, I help clients achieve tremendous and consistent progress toward their bigger goal of putting in place a successful succession or exit plan."

By setting quarterly goals, Brad helps all stakeholders build and keep the momentum moving forward. "The Quarterly Review Stage is the most impactful part of The Succession Solution[SM]. It's during those meetings when we begin the process of helping business owners make more progress with their succession planning over the course of three months than they had achieved in years before starting The Succession Solution[SM]."

As with the Annual Review Stage, in the Quarterly Review Stage, Brad identifies three to five tasks he and my client believe can be accomplished over the next quarter that will move them closer to the annual milestones, which will move them closer to the longer-term goals.

He then helps you assign tasks to people who will be responsible for completing them and reporting back during the next quarterly meeting. Then, at the next quarterly meeting, Brad and the relevant stakeholders meet again to report progress, adjust as needed, and set new goals for the following quarter.

This process repeats every quarter to ensure progress is made and any obstacles are addressed as quickly as possible. And, just like Brian Moran describes in *The 12 Week Year*, Brad notes that many business owners are shocked by how productive they can be in a single quarter when working through The Succession Solution^{SM}. "I tell people that if they're going to take succession planning seriously, they need to meet with me four times throughout the year. After setting big annual and quarterly goals and giving them action steps and accountability, they are frequently surprised by how much progress they are able to make in such a short period of time. In fact, I'll often have business owners come back in just one quarter say, 'Brad, you didn't give us enough. We could have accomplished more.'"

The Human Side of Succession Planning

One of the reasons The Succession Solution^{SM} is so helpful is that it addresses both the technical and human sides of succession planning.

Most professionals fail to address the human side of succession planning. They might be technically adept but underestimate the psychology and emotions of all the relevant stakeholders.

Brad knows and agrees with me that the human side of succession planning is often even more important than the technical or even financial side. "I was recently interviewing executives from a family business that had 68 shareholders and 3 co-CEOs, none of whom were talking to each other," Brad shared. "I had first met with one of the co-CEOs who brought up the subject of succession planning. He explained to me that the other co-CEOs had pushed back against the idea of succession planning because they thought the guy I had spoken to was trying to control the entire situation and wrestle control of the company away from them. Thus, they had objected to the idea of succession planning because they feared losing control."

Less sophisticated or expert planners often view situations like those as hopeless. They think the co-CEOs need to resolve their disputes before a succession plan can be put in place. Using The Succession Solution^{SM} process, Brad quickly discovers all obstacles, human and technical, keeping business owners from creating and executing a succession plan. Then, he uses the six stages of The Succession Solution℠ to make sure all relevant stakeholders are heard and all obstacles are addressed.

"During the first three stages, we are often able to address obstacles that families had thought were unable to be resolved for years," notes Brad. "And with the Annual Review Stage and Quarterly Review Stage, we're able to catch and address additional obstacles that come up during the execution of the plan."

The Devil in the Details

One of the most valuable components of The Succession Solution℠ is how discovery is built into each stage. From the Purpose Stage through the Quarterly Review Stage, Brad is constantly learning what the client has in place, what motivates each key stakeholder, and what obstacles need to be addressed. This helps Brad provide a truly custom solution for each client. It also helps him avoid costly errors and uncover mistakes created by less sophisticated or inexperienced professionals that clients have relied upon in other areas of their business.

"I was recently speaking with a gentleman in a very large organization. He mentioned that he was considering creating two classes of stock at his corporation. After reviewing his company documents, I realized his company wasn't even organized as a corporation and his goal could be achieved much easier than we anticipated. This guy had been running the company for 25 years and hadn't realized that what he thought was formed as a corporation had been formed as a partnership. In this case, it worked out because the partnership model worked in the big picture, and he could achieve his desired outcome very easily. Not all business owners are that lucky, however."

Exit Planning Should Occur as a Part of Succession Planning

As part of a thoughtful succession plan, a business owner may determine it is best to exit or sell the business. However, too many advisors counsel a business owner about exit planning before considering all the options available. Brad believes that while a sale may be appropriate for a business owner, it should not occur until a business owner has gone through some level of succession planning. Too many times Brad has seen a business owner regret the sale of their business based on some particular offer or tax strategy.

There are many valid reasons to sell or exit from a company. This happens frequently in family businesses. A parent starts a company and wants to pass it along to his children, only to discover that none of his children want the company. And it happens in other businesses when the founder has no children and nobody in leadership is ready, willing, and able to take over. In these cases, a succession plan can turn into an exit plan, in which Brad works with other members of my core team and extended network to position your company for a sale to a third party.

The process works in the other direction too. Sometimes, a founder approaches me to sell their business and we discover that the best available deal involves transferring it to others in management.

With Brad and others on my team, we can ensure that all options are on the table when helping our clients achieve their goals. Through The Succession Solution℠ and our greater discovery process, we can often recommend multiple options for the business owner to maximize the value they receive from the company they worked so hard to build.

"Exit planning often works itself out through the succession planning process, and The Succession Solution℠ process is designed to keep all your options open," explains Brad. "For example, if a business owner comes in with blinders on to sell a business, they might end up regretting that decision later on, for several reasons. Unfortunately, many exit planners have only one tool in their toolbox—selling the company to a third party. Those people come in assuming every business needs to be sold. But it can be expensive to sell a business, up to 30 or even 40 percent cost between federal taxes, state taxes, professional fees, broker fees, and other expenses."

These expenses can have a massive negative impact on the business owner's lifestyle. "For example, if you sell a $10 million company that's producing $1 million in net income for the owner, the owner might only end up with $6 million or $7 million after taxes and fees," Brad warns. "The owner would need to achieve a consistent return of 14 to 16 percent on the after-tax sales proceeds to replicate that $1 million in net income. Most advisors would be hard-pressed to generate that type of return most years, which could end up requiring the owner to reduce his lifestyle to avoid depleting the principal."

For this reason, and others, it's critical to work with someone like Brad who understands and can explain all aspects of a business transfer to you. "Exit planning is a natural part of succession planning, but you're putting the cart before the horse if you lead with exit planning," Brad explains. "There are too many moving parts to focus in on one outcome from the beginning, especially when that outcome comes with such high expenses, such as exit planning."

Sometimes, Brad discovers that the right option for all stakeholders is a hybrid approach. "I recently worked with an industrial distributor of HVAC equipment. It's been run by three terrific guys who all got along and ran the company for 30 years. They were always on the same page, except when I met with him about succession planning. Two of them wanted to sell. One of them didn't. So we agreed to go through The Succession Solution℠ to keep their options open."

As part of the process, they brought in an investment banker to explore a potential sale. When the investment banker presented the value of the company on the open market, the partners became depressed. As Brad explains, "They could not afford to sell the business for that price but, for several reasons, transferring it to family members was not an option. So, we continued to work through The Succession Solution℠ and explored a number of options. In the end, we ended up putting together an Employee Stock Ownership Plan, or ESOP. The three partners remained on the board but were able to transfer ownership to their employees at a price that made it a win-win for all involved. This never would have happened if we hadn't gone through the succession planning process. They probably would have sold the company for a whole lot less than they were able to realize while maintaining control and rewarding their employees for their decades of hard work."

With succession planning, the process should lead you to the right solution for achieving the client's goals. Way too many mistakes are made when people put blinders on to pursue a single solution. The Succession Solution^{SM} avoids those disasters, and that's one of the reasons Brad is a core member of my cohesive team.

Sophisticated Estate Planning

Estate planning has never been more difficult for the closely held business owner or high-net-worth individual than it is today. "The estate tax landscape changes much more frequently than it used to," warns Brad. "Over the first 25 years that I practiced law, the federal estate tax exemption remained the same. Over the last 13 years, it's changed 12 times. This has tremendous effects on estate plans. For example, as of 2021, a husband and wife can protect $22 million from estate taxes without breaking a sweat. That amount reduces to just $12 million come 2025 if the laws don't change. So the questions become whether the laws change between 2021 and 2025. This single change wreaks havoc for unsophisticated estate planners who create estate plans under one tax structure and don't keep up with the plan when the laws change."

As Brad explains, however, estate tax laws address just one of three important considerations from an estate planning perspective. "Whenever you're putting together an estate plan, you need to consider much more than just estate taxes," Brad notes. "You need to also address creditors and control issues that arise when someone passes away. But, if you can put together a flexible plan that addresses taxes, creditors, and control, you will have a strong foundation that you can adjust as laws, goals, and family dynamics evolve."

Unfortunately, many less sophisticated professionals let estate taxes rule the estate plan. They know most people don't want to pay more taxes than they have to. However, an estate plan built with that singular goal in mind can often leave assets unprotected from creditors or cause family members to lose control over the assets.

As with other parts of your life, the right solution for you depends on a number of factors and requires coordination and a multidisciplinary approach. That's why my cohesive team and I work in such a well-coordinated fashion to understand exactly what your goals are to minimize taxes, protect your assets, and help your family maintain the right levels of control over your assets.

This coordinated, multidisciplinary approach is important because, when you're doing estate planning, there is often a trade-off between taxes, protection, and control. Sometimes you might save a few dollars in taxes in a way that exposes your assets to creditors. The key is finding the right mix that works for your specific needs. Keeping these three factors in mind and working with a well-coordinated team of experts helps you achieve the right balance.

When Estate Planning Goes Wrong

Sometimes, even experienced estate planners leave their clients in a poor situation.

In one case, Brad discovered one bad result that could have happened due to the lack of coordination among professionals. "I met with an executive of a Fortune 500 company in Pittsburgh, Pennsylvania," Brad shared with me. "He had a net worth in excess of $60 million. He brought in a set of documents that were probably four or five inches thick. And he had what was referred to as a revocable trust because he wanted to avoid probate. He just thought probate was the worst thing in the world, and whoever put together his estate plan helped insulate all of his assets from probate. However, there clearly was no coordination among professionals in his case because I learned through the discovery process that his assets were titled jointly between him and his wife. The assets were never retitled in the name of the revocable trust his lawyer created for him. So, effectively, those trust documents were completely useless because the assets would have passed through probate had we not caught and fixed the issue."

In another situation, Brad was brought in to help after a spouse had to pay $4 million in unnecessary estate taxes and exposure to creditors because of a mistake made by a less sophisticated estate planning attorney. "I was recently introduced to the spouse of a gentleman who had passed away. He was a blue-collar worker who had purchased his company stock as much as he could throughout his career. When he passed away, his stock portfolio had grown to an astounding $20 million. His will directed all stock in his investment accounts to go into a trust for the benefit of his wife, with his brother as the trustee. His wife was not a sophisticated investor, so he wanted to help her manage the portfolio. Additionally, he wanted to make sure his wife was set for life by putting the stock into a trust, thereby protecting it from creditors or others. Unfortunately, the account that held the stock was set up to pass directly to his spouse, not the trust, upon his death, and the stock never made it into the trust. This one, simple mistake cost the spouse about $4 million in taxes and exposed the stock to creditors."

Working with an expert like Brad as part of a well-coordinated team of specialists through my DMMFO helps avoid problems like these and others that arise. Between taxes, creditors, control, or a combination of the three, my team and I help you put together and execute the right estate plan and revisit it as the laws and your personal needs or requirements change.

Keys to Chapter

- According to PwC's Global Family Business Survey 2021, only 30 percent of family businesses have any formalized succession plan, which is up from just 15 percent in 2018. Why does this matter? According to the Family Business Institute, only about 30 percent of family-owned businesses survive into the second generation, with only 12 percent still viable into the third generation, and about 3 percent operating into the fourth generation and beyond.

- Proper succession planning for closely held businesses requires the (1) development, (2) execution, and (3) subsequent review and adjustment of a plan to transfer your business or position in the company to the next generation of managers or owners. Without all three pieces, you, your family, and your business will assume more risk and uncertainty than necessary.

- Attorney Brad Franc and I work closely together with my clients to implement a process Brad developed called The Succession Solution℠, a unique step-by-step process that guides business owners through clearly defined stages before taking specific actions or making final decisions.

- At its core, The Succession Solution℠ works by addressing the four fundamental communities within a company from the start: ownership, governance, leadership, and employment. These four communities matter most to the company's continued viability, and each needs to have clear policies, procedures, and rules in place so everyone in the company is on the same page with respect to roles and responsibilities.

- One of the reasons The Succession Solution℠ is so helpful is that it addresses both the technical and human sides of succession planning. Most professionals fail to address the human side of succession planning. They might be technically adept but underestimate the psychology and emotions of all the relevant stakeholders. Brad and I know that the human side is often more important than even the technical or financial side to many business owners. For example, as part of a thoughtful succession plan, a business owner may determine it is best to exit or sell the business. However, too many advisors counsel a business owner about exit planning before considering all the options available to a business owner.

- Brad and I also help business owners create sophisticated estate plans that help business owners address taxes, creditors, and controls so their business and family are protected both during their lifetime and beyond.

Chapter 15

Establish a World-Class Footer and Foundation for Your Physical and Mental Wellness

Imagine having the same (or even better) level of healthcare that our most conditioned competitive athletes receive to keep their bodies and minds operating at optimal levels in the most competitive environments ...

Having the equivalent of a professional sports team physician and all the tools they have available to them focused on improving *your* physical, mental, and emotional health ...

Having the most cutting-edge tests, tools, and resources at your disposal to take a proactive approach to improving your physical, mental, and emotional health ...

Identifying small issues while they're still small ...

Treating small issues before they become bigger ...

Taking a *proactive* approach to your health ...

Improving your sleep ...

Reducing stress ...

Increasing your energy ...

Optimizing your physical and mental performance ...

Spending more quality time with loved ones …

And even extending your life …

Imagine if you could do all that from anywhere in the world with the best and most complete information available …

What would life be like with that being the reality for you and even your family?

For most people, having a professional sports team physician and their team using the most cutting-edge and sophisticated tools and resources to improve your life would be a pipe dream.

Not for my DiNuzzo Middle-Market Family Office™ clients, though. In fact, although my DMMFO clients come to me talking about improving their business and financial lives, during my discovery process, I learn that the vast majority of them have a strong desire to improve the physical, mental, and emotional health of themselves and their family members.

And, for them, not only can I get them access to a "team physician" level of care but I can even connect them with an actual professional sports team physician to "quarterback" their care: Dr. Mark Anthony Duca, MD, FACP. Even better, because of all the other aspects of my DMMFO, such as by helping improve cash flow and business operations to free you up to work more *on* your business and not *in* your business, I help free up your time so you can spend more quality time with your loved ones and more time improving your physical and mental wellness.

That's where Dr. Duca can come in. Dr. Duca is an internal medicine physician and has headed up the Executive Health Program at UPMC in downtown Pittsburgh for decades.

But Dr. Duca is not just *any* expert-level physician. Dr. Duca has an extensive educational background along with his other career achievements, including acting as a senior aviation medical examiner for the Federal Aviation Administration.

And he was the team physician for the NFL's Pittsburgh Steelers for more than two decades, only recently reducing his role as team physician to an advisory role while he focuses on leading the Executive Health Program at UPMC. In that role, Dr. Duca serves many of my DMMFO clients, many of whom travel from all over the country to spend the day with Dr. Duca and his team to establish a world-class footer and foundation for success starting with their physical and mental wellness.

Finally, Dr. Duca is also my personal physician. Like many of the specialists on my cohesive team and extended network whom I make available to my DMMFO clients, I don't just talk the talk. I use the services of the specialists who help me achieve my personal goals as well. For example, I have personally enjoyed the Executive Health Physical at UPMC that my DMMFO clients get to experience when they visit Dr. Duca. In fact, I am on a complete Executive Health Physical Plan, which I will discuss later in this chapter, and can attest to the positive impact that establishing a world-class footer and foundation for your physical and mental wellness under his care can have on all aspects of your business and personal life.

Dr. Duca is one of the very few physicians in the country who provide this level of proactive, comprehensive care to their patients. And he can seamlessly coordinate with physicians and other specialists all around the country to help with any follow-up or additional specialized care so my DMMFO clients can build upon the findings and suggestions by Dr. Duca and his team from the comfort of their own home, virtually, or by visiting local specialists in coordination with Dr. Duca.

How Health Optimization Expert and Specialist Dr. Mark Duca Helps Improve the Lives of Clients, Their Families, and Their Businesses

The typical relationship between a patient and the healthcare system is heavy on treatment and light on prevention.

Specifically, an annual physical typically lasts between 30 and 60 minutes, only a fraction of which is spent with the physician. It typically begins with a nurse measuring your blood pressure, heart rate, temperature, and a few other vital signs. After checking vital signs, the nurse or doctor will ask you to update your health history. The doctor will then physically examine you to identify any obvious medical issues.

Depending on your health history and other factors, the doctor might also order some basic bloodwork. Typically, this would include a "complete blood count" and a "complete metabolic panel." The complete blood count evaluates your blood platelets and red and white blood cells to check for infections, inflammation, several common conditions, and your ability to form blood clots. The complete metabolic panel checks your liver and kidney health, blood sugar and protein, and a few other body functions and processes. It can identify several conditions including liver problems, diabetes, and kidney failure.

You may also receive certain additional basic screening tests for certain conditions based on gender, age, and any known risk factors.

Although there is nothing inherently "wrong" with the typical approach, Dr. Mark Duca does much more for me and my clients. His services are one important part of a two-part footer and foundation of physical, mental, and emotional healthcare. In the next chapter, I will introduce the second part, which builds upon what Dr. Duca and his team do to help you continue to improve your physical, mental, and emotional health to levels many don't think are even possible.

"Our focus is on prevention, being proactive, and conducting effective follow-up" Dr. Duca explains. "We want to identify current problems, potential problems, and risk factors as early as possible to have a head start on issues, even before they develop, if possible. We like to be very, very proactive in our preventative health approach."

When it comes to follow-up, Dr. Duca doesn't just send you test results that indicate what measures fall in and out of the "normal" range. He walks you through exactly what he has seen from your entire time in the office and helps you make the best, most informed decisions about next steps.

"We don't just send a whole bunch of data and leave the patient to research what it all means. It's very, very important to have open communication with our clients about their health, so we review the results with them in great detail through whatever mode they prefer. We then make recommendations to them about what we suggest for treatment and preventative issues," Dr. Duca explains.

Dr. Duca makes sure each patient has enough information to follow up on what's most important to them wherever they prefer, too. "Ultimately, it's the patient's decision about where and when they would like to do any follow-up," says Dr. Duca. "The overwhelming majority of our patients will follow up with us because they're very comfortable with us, along with data, communication, and presentation. But we make sure each patient has enough information that they can follow up wherever they are most comfortable. Because many people fly to Dr. Duca's facility from around the world, some patients choose to visit physicians in their area for some conditions while others come back to us, either in person or virtually."

Dr. Duca's "proactive, prevention, and follow-up" approach looks much different from what most patients are used to experiencing. He goes several layers deeper in each step of the process and spends much more time with patients to make sure he can use the best and latest medical science across all areas of discipline to identify and address as many physical, mental, and emotional conditions as possible.

"I take great pride in our Executive Health Program being a comprehensive program based on the best and latest medical guidelines," says Dr. Duca. "We take great care to be at the cutting edge of medical science. In doing so, I can make recommendations based only on established guidelines and well-established scientific protocols. The backbone of our program is based on the most up-to-date medical research and guidelines."

At the core of the Executive Health Program and all the benefits of taking a proactive prevention approach, lies the *Executive Health Physical*.

Treat Your Wellness like You Treat Your Business by Upgrading to an Executive Health Physical Plan

The difference between having a typical physical and having an annual Executive Health Physical is night and day.

For starters, the Executive Health Physical begins before the day of your appointment. "I like to have some information about each patient before they get to my office, so we'll send them an information packet to find out about their history, medications, and any particular interest or questions they have. Before the appointment, I review this information before they come in so I have an idea of what I need to look for, what they are concerned about, questions they may have, or what current conditions they may have. I also encourage people to write a list of questions down to bring with them to the appointment so we can make sure we cover everything they wanted to cover. I can't tell you how many times people walk in without a list and forget their concerns," says Dr. Duca.

Patients then choose from either a half- or full-day appointment in-office. At the beginning of the appointment, Dr. Duca and his staff will sit down with the patient and go through a detailed history with them. Dr. Duca will review their questionnaire with them along with past medical history, family history, medications, allergies, and any other pertinent information.

Unlike typical annual physicals, once Dr. Duca has collected the information he needs, he lets the patient direct the next phase of the appointment. "I like to let the patient drive the bus," Dr. Duca explains. "They're coming to us. They are often coming in with a specific goal. They may have specific questions. So instead of me going through a standard template with each patient, I like the patient to direct the conversation at this point and ask any questions they may have upfront. When they're done, I'll go back in and backfill to make sure we're covering all the bases. But I always lead with the patient's concerns. Once we complete this part of the exam, I conduct a detailed physical examination from head to toe."

Although the prework, history, and physical exam are more detailed and thorough than the typical experience, some of the greatest differentiators and benefits of Dr. Duca's Executive Health Physical over the typical annual physicals come from what happens next.

"After we complete the history and physical exam, we conduct thorough bloodwork and other tests, which we tailor to each patient's individual preference and what I believe is indicated," Dr. Duca explains. "All of that testing gets done on-site, here." Dr. Duca has a wide array of services on-site. Dr. Duca shared some of those services with me, including to the extent the patient wants or needs these services:

- X-ray services
- body fat analyses
- DEXA scanning for bone density
- a very high-quality vision and audio testing center for patients
- a wide array of cardiovascular diagnostics that oftentimes will serve as a backbone of someone's evaluation
- echocardiography (which is also interpreted on-site)
- cardiopulmonary stress testing
- nuclear stress tests
- spirometry
- additional testing that is specific to males or females (such as mammography, gynecologic examinations, among other options, if female patients desire)
- detailed testosterone level and other male-specific services
- the availability of both male and female physicians if a patient has a preference

In addition, patients can experience several other ancillary services during their time with Dr. Duca if they desire, including the following:

- a counselor for stress management
- a nutritionist
- a detailed fitness analysis in partnership with the Health and Fitness Center at the Duquesne Club
- certified athletic trainers
- a detailed fitness analysis conducted by certified exercise physiologists
- spending the whole day, if they desire, even eating lunch at the Duquesne Club and taking advantage of other services at the club, such as taking a steam or shower or other ancillary services.

About a week after your appointment, Dr. Duca and his team send you a detailed, plain-English report and follow up with you to discuss it in detail. "Patients are free to take that information to another facility, follow up with us, or do nothing and simply keep my report for their records," Dr. Duca explains. "Receiving your results and report and your discussion with me is all part of the program. We follow up with you however works best for you, as well. I leave it open-ended on how the patient would like to follow up, whether they like the follow-up via phone call, via email, Zoom, or some other way. Communication is very, very important to our program, and we make sure that the proper follow-up happens so patients can receive the full value of all we do with them."

Benefits of Upgrading to an Executive Health Physical Plan

When it comes to all aspects of our healthcare, we can get the best results by being intentional and controlling what we can control. That's true in our business and our personal lives. And there's no easier way to control more of your healthcare than by upgrading to having an annual Executive Health Physical Plan instead of the typical 30-to-60-minute, basic-level diagnosis and treatment physical.

Going from 30 to 60 minutes and basic diagnostics and treatment to an annual Executive Health Physical provides a number of benefits, even beyond the obvious. Take the difference between the typical cholesterol or cardiovascular risk screening, for example:

We put a big emphasis on not only looking at the total choles-terol numbers and doing somebody's risk stratification but also on what is called lipoprotein subfractionation. The typical cholesterol screening lets people know their total cholesterol numbers. Those numbers are important, but we also break down the components of the lipid profile. We also do cardiac biomarkers and ancillary testing that can help us identify risks. For example, coronary cal-cium scores and cardiovascular stress testing are two things that are not typically done in a routine physical examination when evaluating a cholesterol profile. By going deeper in our analysis and conducting additional testing relating to risk factors, we are often able to reveal increased risk long before what is possible with a typical physical.

Dr. Duca shared one recent example of how this depth of testing can impact patients, changing some of the personal details of the patient to protect their identity:

A middle-aged male recently came in for an Executive Health Physical. In his pre-appointment intake, we learned that he had a strong family history of premature coronary disease and had generally kept up with periodic physical examinations. He had had his cholesterol checked four or five years earlier, didn't exercise very much, and was probably 10 or 15 pounds overweight.

When he came in, he showed me the lipid profile they received at his last annual physical. It didn't look too bad. His total cholesterol was a little over 200 and his LDL cholesterol was about 140.

With his family history, I knew the detailed subfractionation testing would be critical for this patient because it doesn't just measure total cholesterol numbers but also measures LDL and HDL particle size. LDL particle size, in particular, is very important for a patient with this family history because of how coronary plaque forms. There are little spaces in the walls of the coronary arteries. The smaller the LDL particle size, the easier it is for them to fit in the walls of the coronary arteries and start to build the foundation for a cholesterol plaque. Thus, having a significantly elevated number of small LDL particles is a big risk factor that we look at when we do this subfractionation.

When we got the results back from our testing, we learned that this patient had a small LDL particle quantification that was off the charts.

We also conducted serum cardiac biomarkers and cardiac inflammatory biomarkers and found pretty significant abnormalities.

Based on these results, we were able to intervene much earlier than would have happened had he waited for the basic testing to become concerning.

Having experienced both traditional physicals and Dr. Duca's Executive Health Physical, the immediate benefits of early identification and the proactive approach are instantly noticeable. For example, the difference in the information from the blood tests alone feels like the difference between looking at myself in the mirror versus looking at myself through a microscope. I see surface-level issues in one and molecular-level issues in another.

"I'm not aware of anyone in the general medicine field who does this level of analysis on a routine basis," Dr. Duca explains. "This level of thoroughness and detail is something our program does. It may be something a cardiologist would do with respect to cardiovascular concerns. It may be something that a lipidologist, which is somebody who specializes in the analysis and management of lipid abnormalities, would look at. But this is not something routinely done by the vast majority of medical providers."

For these reasons, and more, many clients choose to upgrade their healthcare experience to having an annual Executive Health Physical. That level of thoroughness and depth of care helps catch—and control—many issues while they are still minor. And that helps you lift and strengthen the overall foundation of your health, giving you even more opportunities to optimize your health, performance, and energy using some of the biohacking and other options available through my DMMFO. As in any area of your life, if you control what you can control, you will be in much better shape. And with Executive Health Physicals and some of the other healthcare experts on my team, you can control much more than many people know about. I'll talk about two of my clients' favorite biohacking options later in this book to show you just some of what's possible.

Genetic Testing and Other Cutting-Edge Science

Imagine being able to identify cancer risk before the cancer develops. Advances in genetic testing have made that possible in certain circumstances. That's why Dr. Duca and his team have begun offering genetic testing through their executive medicine program.

"This is an area that is still in its infancy stage, but we are keeping on the cutting edge," Dr. Duca says. "Currently, not only do we provide the testing we also provide the counseling to interpret the testing and have enrolled the genetics counselor at UPMC Magee-Womens Hospital. One area that genetic testing has been helpful with is identifying potential cancers early on. We've been able to talk with patients about increased risks for a certain kind of cancer and discuss whether there is anything we can do to mitigate that risk."

Genetic testing is just one example of how Dr. Duca and his team stay on the cutting edge in their proactive, preventative approach to your health.

Early Identification and Intervention

As Dr. Duca emphasized, getting all this information about your body has numerous benefits. Perhaps the most impactful benefit involves early identification and intervention with life-threatening diseases.

Take another patient who visited Dr. Duca a few years back, for example. At the time, he was a high-level executive chairman in the business world. He visited Dr. Duca for an Executive Health Physical.

After completing the intake, Dr. Duca asked the patient his typical open-ended question, "What would you like to talk about today?" The patient responded with several concerns, including that he had been feeling really tired for a while. During the course of his examination, an X-ray also revealed an abnormality. The next day, the blood test results were returned, and they revealed that the patient had acute leukemia, which would not have been identified without that level of testing.

"We had this patient admitted to UPMC Hillman Cancer Center within 48 hours to begin chemotherapy for his acute leukemia," explained

Dr. Duca. "He did very well and ended up having a successful stem cell transplant. He is now retired and enjoying his life. That's just one example of many that he was very, very fortunate that we saw him when we did."

More Energy, Less Stress, and Better Days

Although Executive Health Physicals can help identify and address big issues to help you extend your healthy life, those are not the only benefits you can experience through executive healthcare. You can also experience day-to-day benefits that make those extra days more productive and enjoyable.

"A lot of our male patients come to us feeling run down, stressed out, constantly tired, not very motivated, and talking about other symptoms people associate with being a successful, busy, middle-aged man," says Dr. Duca. "While these symptoms can indicate life-threatening conditions, such as leukemia, other times, the cause involves low testosterone levels. Many doctors will recognize this as a possible testosterone-level issue. If they discover that to be the case, they will intervene to boost testosterone levels. While that's important and helpful, we take it a few steps further to work with patients to optimize their health."

More energy, less stress, and better days are just some of the benefits Dr. Duca and his team can help people achieve if they are suffering from low testosterone levels. Of course, like with the cholesterol and heart health testing, Dr. Duca and his team take a thorough, holistic approach with men who want to optimize their physical conditioning:

> There's a tremendous amount of confusion regarding testosterone levels and supplementation and a lot of it is physician driven. As men age, their conditions and symptoms tend to progress on a gradual level. Oftentimes, patients have heard different advice from their physician than what our testing reveals. That's why it's so important for me to give them my evaluation and not just the raw data. Ultimately, the patient makes the final decisions as far as what they want to do for any intervention. We see ourselves as

a resource to them to help them make informed decisions about their healthcare.

Treating Your Body like You Treat Your Business

If your body were a business, how would you treat it? Would you hire someone who took just a surface-level approach in checking for issues that could destroy your business next year, 5 years, or even 10 years down the road? Would you want partial information about your sales? Would you hire a consultant who came in for 30 minutes and told you everything was fine?

Or would you want the best-of-the-best working for you? Would you want cutting-edge science and technology on your side? Would you want to take a proactive approach to identifying issues before they get big? Would you want to spend an entire day with an expert consultant who has access to the best-of-the-best specialists in their field if something specific comes up?

If we all treated our bodies like we treat our businesses, I'm confident we would take a more proactive approach with our healthcare. And executive medicine through Dr. Duca and his team can give you that level of care and attention—the level of care and attention you deserve.

Keys to Chapter

- In business, there's only so much you can achieve with partial information and limited sets of tools. The same is true with medical care.
- When your care is limited to what insurance providers decide is necessary, your providers limit the tests they perform, the tools they make available, and the time they spend with you. Your care becomes dictated by health insurance company profits. Your care becomes reactive, conducting basic testing and treating issues only when they surface into symptoms. Even then, your treatment is often limited to addressing symptoms and not resolving underlying issues.

- With an Executive Health Physical, your physical and mental health decisions are made by you and your healthcare provider based on your full medical history, health goals, and significantly more detailed information. Treatment is then provided in a proactive manner with more complete information and a virtually limitless set of tools.

- Upgrading to an annual Executive Health Physical Plan gives you the most detailed and sophisticated information available about your physical and mental health to raise the footer and foundation of your physical, mental, and emotional health.

- With the information gained from a single Executive Health Physical, many successful middle-market business owners can proactively identify (and resolve) underlying health issues long before they lead to significant symptoms, improving energy levels, raising their overall physical, mental, and emotional health, and addressing small health issues while they are still small and able to be resolved.

- The difference between the typical healthcare plan and an Executive Health Physical Plan can literally be the difference between life and death.

Chapter 16

Level Up Your Executive Health Physical through Expert Delivery of Concierge Medicine

With your footer and foundation of physical, mental, and emotional health in place from an Executive Health Physical Plan, what comes next? What do you do with all the detailed information you learn about your body and mind during your Executive Health Physical? Between Dr. Duca and his team and additional members of my team of specialists, your options are virtually limitless. And because much of what my team and I do can be done virtually, receiving proactive, personalized, and continued care to further improve your physical, mental, and emotional health is easier than ever.

Daniel Carlin, MD's professional dedication to human health and the human body began in 1981 when he graduated from Carnegie Mellon University with a double degree in chemistry and philosophy. After graduation, he enrolled in Tufts University School of Medicine, where he earned his MD in 1985. After graduation, he became the medical officer on board the USS *Mississippi*, completed a general surgery internship at Bethesda Naval Hospital, learned field medicine at the US Armed Forces Combat

Casualty Care School, and completed his residency in emergency medicine at Columbia University College of Physicians and Surgeons. He is a board-certified emergency physician and a former US Navy medical officer.

After a decade of practicing in several demanding healthcare environments, Dr. Carlin decided to take a different direction with his career. His goal in doing so was to restore integrity to healthcare, in the company of great colleagues, for as many people as possible. That remains his mission with medicine to this day.

A lot of advancements have been made in human health, the human body, and the provision of medical care since Dr. Carlin graduated from medical school, and he has been at the forefront of a lot of the advancements the world benefits from today. For example, Dr. Carlin has become a national leader in the field of telemedicine and a recognized pioneer in the delivery of medical care to distant populations.

As a result of the continuous innovation and advancements Dr. Carlin has made in his practice and to the medical community as a whole, he has become a frequent speaker to medical and international development audiences. He has spoken at institutions such as the MIT Media Lab and the United States Naval Academy, and professional conferences such as the American Telemedicine Association and the International Development Council.

His work has been featured in *Business Week*, *Forbes*, *Fortune*, the *Financial Times*, the *New York Times*, the *Wall Street Journal*, and *Worth*. He has also been a guest speaker on *The Today Show*, *Dateline NBC*, and *The Oprah Winfrey Show*. And he is a core member of the DiNuzzo Middle-Market Family Office™ cohesive team of specialists working to improve the lives of all my clients.

How Concierge Medicine Expert and Specialist Dr. Dan Carlin Helps Change the Lives of Clients, Their Families, and Their Businesses

What if you choose among doctors the same way you work with a concierge at a hotel to choose among activities on a vacation?

The concierge takes the time to learn all about your family, what you like, what you don't like, and helps you identify the best activities for your unique needs.

Dan Carlin and his team at WorldClinic are those concierges for you and your family, only with respect to your health and lifestyle, not activities on vacation. Dr. Carlin founded WorldClinic in 1998 as a private, proactive, concierge medicine practice that uses telemedicine to care for a diverse client base of organizations, senior executives, and individuals and their families.

Functioning as a personal virtual emergency room and healthcare concierge, WorldClinic's physicians and care team provide immediate telemedical emergency response and urgent, chronic condition management on an on-demand, anytime, anywhere basis.

They give their members immediate access to the WorldClinic physician group and care team, allowing them to deliver a proactive, comprehensive care model that places their members at the center of all of their efforts. Additionally, like other members of my well-coordinated, cohesive team of specialists, Dr. Carlin works closely with other healthcare professionals on my team and any existing healthcare professionals you may have to ensure you get the best available care.

Welcome to the world of concierge medicine, which provides integrated healthcare and prevention measures anywhere and anytime. Being able to refer you to incredible concierge medicine service providers, such as Dr. Carlin, is another benefit available to DMMFO clients who want access to custom and innovative healthcare options. And just like with all services I help my clients access, only clients who use Dr. Carlin's services incur that cost. Moreover, as with all of the healthcare introductions we make for our clients, DMMFO doesn't make a dime. We work to understand what our clients' goals and priorities are and present them with options to consider, including people like Dr. Duca, Dr. Carlin, and other specialized options. The client then decides which, if any, they will work with and enter into those relationships directly with the provider.

Successful business owners and affluent family stewards work hard building their businesses and leading their families. Without the effectiveness and convenience of people like Dr. Carlin and his team, many people let the hectic nature of their days cause them to delay much-needed medical care for months or even years. Throughout that time, their business grows but their bodies slowly break down. Their physical health suffers. Their mental health suffers. Their energy wanes. Being under the care of a team like Dr. Carlin's brings the best healthcare to you, wherever you are and whenever you need it. No need to drive to their office. They have mastered the art and science of telemedicine and coordinating care on your terms.

The customized, proactive manner in which Dr. Carlin and others on my healthcare team work together to help lift and optimize the health of my clients and their families is one of the best examples of my DMMFO core values at work. This isn't the typical telemedicine we all come across today. This is a proactive, expert, high-touch group of specialists committed to helping you live a longer, healthier, more enjoyable life.

After experiencing the level of care, expertise, and attention they receive from Dr. Duca, Dr. Carlin, and some of our biohacking experts, many individuals have commented about how deep, personal, and customized our approach is for their and their family members' physical, mental, and emotional wellness. Each time they do, I am reminded of the impact I can have on my clients' lives by helping them in each area of their lives—from personal and business risk management to business growth and income tax savings to family goals and improved health. My team and I work together with the sole focus of optimizing all aspects of your life. And there are few areas in which we help clients that get as much positive feedback as the impact my healthcare and biohacking team members have made in people's lives.

How Personalized, Proactive Concierge Medicine Is Different

After spending 20 years in the emergency room, Dr. Carlin noticed a problem. "What I was seeing was a degradation in primary care and prevention," says Dr. Carlin, "We started out in a place where it was all about crisis and keeping people alive for the next hour," he says.

What happens when a medical team only focuses on acute care and only for a short period of time? They make short-term decisions that sometimes cause other problems. Of course, in an emergency setting, you make the best decisions you can under the circumstances, but all that short-term focus for all those years took a toll on Dr. Carlin.

"Now, with WorldClinic, at least half our energy is going into keeping people alive 15, 20, 30 years from now. We focus on getting them the preventative and primary care they need to live a long, healthy life."

Working with DMMFO clients allows Dr. Carlin to continue to focus on the most important part of WorldClinic's services: deepening the relationship between the doctor and the patient. "If you've got a strong relationship with your doctor, that physician is going to be there for you when you need them," says Dr. Carlin. "You get more time to listen to the patient and avoid reducing complex medical issues to a simple algorithm," which is what many private practice physicians do, explains Dr. Carlin. In some practices, when you tell your physician your symptoms, you can watch your doctor enter your symptoms into a computer. When the physician enters the symptoms in the computer, the computer spits out the course of care for the physician to follow.

Years ago, the concept of a physician building a relationship with their patient would not have seemed so revolutionary. Unfortunately, it is today. And combined with staying on the cutting edge of both medical care and medical technology plus access to some of the most highly skilled and experienced physicians who all take a proactive approach to improving your health and extending your life, Dr. Carlin helps DMMFO clients achieve the best in care and convenience.

As Dr. Carlin puts it, "You get better medical care."

Personality Profiles of Healthy WorldClinic Patients

Visits with the doctor become a lot more fun when you're healthy and the doctors are like Dr. Carlin, excited to perform preventive care to help you live your best life. Two personality types dominate about 95 percent of WorldClinic's patients, he explains:

1. people who pay close attention to their health and treat their lifespan like they treat assets in an investment portfolio, and
2. people who don't pay attention to their health.

"Category one is the folks who are paying attention and treating their lifespan like assets in their portfolio," he says. "They're engaging and managing, and they're really fun to work with because they're taking it seriously." Dr. Carlin will examine their metrics with numerous and broad screening tests, and then specific ones that are appropriate in your specific situation. In other environments, that level of bloodwork is basically unheard of. But Dr. Carlin knows that understanding what's going on inside your body can help you in many ways. For example, it can reveal any issues sooner than waiting for external symptoms to arise. It can also provide a level of detail about your health that can help Dr. Carlin and his team work to optimize your health.

For example, one business owner with whom Dr. Carlin recently worked had spent his entire life worrying about his heart health due to having a high risk of heart disease. Working completely virtually, Dr. Carlin was able to dig deep into his underlying health issues, mitigate that risk, and create a meaningful positive benefit for the patient.

"We're going to have a happy outcome with that patient," says Dr. Carlin. "He's looked at his life and said, about his heart health, 'This is the most important thing—it's more important than money,'" he explains. "Working completely virtually, we were able to address issues he has been worried about his entire adult life. I'm confident we just extended his healthy life by about 16 years. That means he will have 16 more healthy years to do whatever he wants—building his companies, leading his teams, doing philanthropy, and, most importantly, being present and healthy for his wife and children."

"The second personality type is the people who don't pay very much attention to their health," says Dr. Carlin. "They generally trust their doctors to watch out for them and figure their hospitals will take care of them when they get sick. They go to the nearest doctor if they go at all. And they either trust that they are doing fine, until something major happens, or they secretly worry about their health but do nothing about it."

"I can't think of a more destructive, costly, invalid assumption than the assumption that your hospital will take care of you," says Dr. Carlin. "Don't assume anything. For the longest time, people have assumed someone else was going to take care of their healthcare. They never do, especially if they don't take the time to truly get to know you. You truly can add years to your life when you take a proactive approach to your health."

Dr. Carlin's processes ensure that every patient is given the most actively managed healthcare available. From the tests they perform as a matter of course to the availability and convenience of receiving expert treatment, Dr. Carlin works hard to help you reach your peak physical, mental, and emotional health. You can find first-rate preventive and acute care anytime, anywhere, at home, or abroad. "Even if you're six time zones away, traveling in a faraway country, it's irrelevant to the level of care you will receive. Our door is always open," says Dr. Carlin. WorldClinic is there literally as a 24/7, minute-by-minute service dedicated to your and your family's health.

 Keys to Chapter

- Successful business owners and affluent family stewards work hard building their businesses and leading their families. Without the effectiveness and convenience of concierge medicine, many people let the hectic nature of their days cause them to delay much-needed medical care for months or even years.

- Concierge medicine provides integrated healthcare and prevention measures anywhere and anytime, helping busy business owners get access to top healthcare services on their schedule.

- Concierge medicine allows successful middle-market business owners to focus on issues beyond diagnosing and treating disease. For example, Dr.

Dan Carlin and his team at WorldClinic spend at least half their energy on longevity and quality of life, seeking to customize their care to help their patients live a long, healthy life.

- The typical concierge medicine patient is someone who either (1) pays close attention to their health and treats their lifespan like they treat assets in an investment portfolio, or (2) *doesn't* pay much attention to their health. Many people in these categories can benefit from all the convenience and expertise available to them through concierge medicine.

- The best concierge medicine options ensure that every patient is given the most actively managed healthcare available. From the tests they perform as a matter of course to the availability and convenience of receiving expert treatment, the right concierge medicine provider will work hard to help you reach your peak physical, mental, and emotional health no matter how busy you are or where in the world you are located.

PART 4:

Biohacking: Taking Mental and Physical Wellness to an Even Higher Level for Those Who Want It

---

Chapter 17

Health and Fitness Biohacking to Maximize Your Body's Energy and Improve Your Physical and Mental Quality of Life

After beefing up the footer and foundation of their health through an Executive Health Physical Plan and adding a concierge medicine team to continue to build upon the physical and mental health foundations, some of my clients want to continue to elevate their physical and mental health. They are enjoying the many benefits of Executive Health Physical Plans and concierge medicine and want to do even more for their health, including elevating their energy, improving their sleep, and even extending their life.

Like other areas of specialty, when a client expresses a desire to improve a certain area of their life, that's where my extended network comes into play. Some people want to *really* take their physical, mental, and emotional health to the next level. That's where biohacking and other next-level body and mind specialists in my network can help. Of course, like with many other specialists, I don't make a penny referring clients to these specialists. My clients work directly with these specialists to the extent they want to. But helping clients achieve the highest level of physical, mental, and emotional wellness is a core part of helping clients discover, create, and *live* their Best-Life™—a core value and benefit of my DiNuzzo Middle-Market Family Office™.

For the sake of brevity, I won't discuss *all* the "next-level" options available to improve health and extend living years. But I'll introduce you to two common on-demand services that some of my clients request. These types of services are delivered on-demand or by request from my clients who have specialized goals. Like other services, the client pays for them only when they use them. And only clients who want these types of specialized services receive them.

The two examples I will share with you here both fall into the healthcare or biohacking arena, namely health and fitness and anti-aging biohacking options. These are just two of many biohacking experts I have on my team and in my network, each with different areas of specialty and expertise. But they are two useful examples of the level of specialized care I am able to help my clients access.

The first example of the next-level health options I'll share here is Peter Z. Wasowski and the work he is doing to help people improve sleep, maximize energy, achieve better hormonal balance, and accomplish an overall higher quality of life. Peter is the founder and CEO of Vasper Systems. A native of Poland, Peter moved to the U.S. in 1962 at age 13. Since then, he has amassed over 48 years of experience in the field of medical technology and vascular health, including working at Siemens, GE Medical Systems, and with Steve Jobs after Jobs was fired from Apple.

Later, Peter founded his own company, CoolSystems, Inc., where he helped create Game Ready™, an active compression and cold therapy recovery system that has become the industry standard in professional sports care and rehabilitation.

Throughout his professional career, Peter has earned a reputation for developing innovative technologies to improve results in the healthcare, fitness, and human performance arenas. For example, in his early 20s, Peter worked with a leading neurosurgeon to develop a new piece of equipment that allowed doctors to identify brain tumors in one day instead of over six to eight weeks. At the time, identifying brain tumors required two invasive procedures conducted six to eight weeks apart. During that time, tumors would continue to grow, often to the point where they were inoperable or no longer treatable. Peter's equipment allowed doctors to conduct both procedures only 45 minutes apart, saving precious time and improving outcomes for patients.

Peter has continued to apply the same innovative, problem-solving approach to other healthcare, fitness, and human performance challenges throughout his career, fusing his extensive knowledge and ever-growing experience with his passion for expanding human wellness. Peter's inventions, including the Vasper System, which I discuss in more detail below, are used by the U.S. military, Stanford University, UCSF, UMASS, Olympic and professional athletes, physicians, and countless individuals from around the world.

And Peter is also a member of my cohesive team of specialists who help me optimize my clients' physical, mental, and emotional health.

How Vasper, along with Physiology Expert and Human Performance Specialist Peter Wasowski, Helps Change the Lives of Clients, Their Families, and Their Businesses

As we get older, a number of things start happening in our bodies, including a decline in our natural production of hormones, such as testosterone, estrogen, growth hormone, and even melatonin. This is important because hormones are our bodies' natural support system for many of our organs and systems.

"Your hormone levels are naturally dropping," explains Peter. "In fact, every 10 years after puberty, there is a significant reduction in the stimulation of the pituitary gland that produces a number of hormones. This causes us to lose bone tissue, muscle tissue, and take longer to recover from aches and pains, among other effects," he continues.

Most people think of aches and pains, decreased performance, lower energy, and other common experiences of getting older as the natural aging process. But what if they don't *have* to be?

If you go to a doctor and they test your hormone levels and discover they are low, what are they going to say? Most likely they'll tell you "Your hormone levels are normal for your age; you're just getting older." The truth is our hormones do not decline because we age; we age because our hormones decline.

Through his latest invention, the Vasper System, Peter helps my clients address the "natural" decline in hormone production and slow down or even reverse many of the effects of aging that traditional medicine tells you to live with for those who choose to purchase, lease, or access a locally available Vasper System device.

Basically, what we're doing is bio-mimicking the physiology that naturally occurs in children. Children tend to have a very high concentration of lactic acid in their muscles. This is true for a number of reasons. First, children have a higher natural level of growth hormones because they are still growing. Their pituitary gland needs to produce growth hormone for them to grow. Second, children are almost always moving at full speed. All that running around produces an exercise effect, which, again, triggers growth hormone secretion. Third, they are small. All the lactic acid that builds up from the exercise effect is spread across smaller muscles. Together, these factors result in very highly concentrated lactic acid in their muscles.

The keyword here is "concentration," of lactic acid not the amount of lactic acid. The concentration is what drives a very powerful signal to the pituitary gland, to the brain, requesting growth hormone to rebuild those muscles back to pre-exercise conditions. Children do that naturally, on top of their higher baseline production of growth hormones because they're growing. They boost those hormone levels.

This is one of the reasons why a child is such a resilient being. If you bring a child to a doctor with a meniscus tear or ligament tear, most of the time there's really no medical intervention necessary. The child recovers very quickly on their own. Once you hit puberty, your body is taller already and you have bigger muscles for the lactic acid to spread around. You can no longer concentrate lactic acid to the same levels because those muscles are longer. You also don't have time to run around all day. You're sitting in school and coming home to do hours of homework. Your natural hormone secretions start slowing down. Because of those three things, every 10 years, we lose 14 percent of our, what's called, anabolic hormones, the hormones that rebuild our body.

Whether you want to enhance physical performance, need rehabilitation or recovery from injury, or increase overall health and wellness, Peter and the Vasper System can help give you a natural boost that makes you look and feel better than you have in years.

As I discuss in more detail below, the effects of using the Vasper System build off one another too. For example, the most frequently reported benefit is improved sleep. That alone causes a number of positive benefits to your physical and mental health, as well as in your business. As explained, below, the Vasper System does much more than *just* improve sleep.

Creating the Vasper System Out of Necessity

"Necessity is the mother of invention."— **English proverb**

Peter's years of innovation in the health and human performance arenas built him a solid reputation across the business and sports worlds. In one of his first big forays into professional sports, Peter created a product currently known as Game Ready, which helped alleviate one of the biggest problems in professional sports: recovery.

No matter how fine-tuned a professional athlete's body becomes, injuries happen. When they happen on the road, even a minor injury can linger due to the nature of travel. "Most airplane cabins are pressurized to

8,000 feet above sea level," explains Peter. "Flying at that altitude can cause an inflammatory response to an injured athlete. This means even a small injury can linger or worsen if they have to get on a plane to travel home."

Peter witnessed athletes having injuries worsen so badly on flights that they would need to be carried off the plane, even if they had walked onto the plane on their own. Like he has done so many times during his career, Peter saw this as an opportunity to solve a big problem. "We designed a piece of equipment that could actually treat the injury in flight using a combination of cryotherapy and compression. Even though the plane was at altitude, the cooling and compression created from the device would lower the anabolic rate and cause broken blood vessels to come together. At the end of the flight, the athlete would be better than before they got on the plane."

Peter sold the device under the name CoolSystems until he sold the company at age 50 to the famous sports agent Leigh Steinberg, whose life inspired the movie *Jerry Maguire*.

Having cashed out of the business world at age 50, Peter happily retired to Hawaii with his wife and children. He spent the next few years living in paradise. Unlike his wife and children, however, Peter wasn't able to enjoy all that Hawaii had to offer because of two significant health challenges.

The first challenge Peter was dealing with was traumatic arthritis in his ankles. He had broken both of his ankles in separate accidents, and, over the years, it developed into what's called traumatic arthritis:

> Being in the tropics was definitely difficult for me because it caused me to suffer from inflammation and swelling of the joints. I was in a lot of pain—and on a lot of pain medications. I remember getting up at night trying to make it to the bathroom and having to crawl on my hands and knees because I couldn't put any weight on my ankles. After a while, I thought about living the rest of my life this way and thought to myself that it was no way to

live. And I was only 50 years old. It wasn't going to get any better. It would only have gotten worse.

In addition to traumatic arthritis, Peter was also prediabetic. His grandfather died from diabetes, and he was about to have to start taking insulin. "Once you get on insulin, your life spirals down because you're basically married to it for a long time—sometimes for the rest of your life," Peter notes. "So I wanted to design something that addresses the root cause, rather than treat symptoms of my diabetes, while at the same time improving my arthritis in my ankles."

For one device to achieve both seemingly unrelated goals, Peter had to invent a device that would improve his underlying health and wouldn't just target his blood sugar or joints. He needed to improve how his entire body functioned at the base level.

He basically benefited from his years and years of experience of working in medicine and created a very crude prototype of a piece of equipment in the lab behind his house that combined what he now refers to as VC3 Biohack Technology—compression, liquid cooling, and circulation. He never intended for the equipment to do anything beyond help with his arthritis and prediabetic state but after using the device for just two short weeks, he noticed so many benefits that his plans began to shift:

> I designed a very crude prototype in the lab behind my house, and after using the prototype for about two weeks, I noticed that the pain in my ankles was gone. Two or three weeks later, I took my first glucose tolerance test to check my blood sugar levels, and for the first time in 41 years, it was normal. I knew I was onto something and that this device I threw together in my home lab could help a lot of people.
>
> That realization changed everything for me. I went from happily retired without even thinking about getting back in the business world to obsessed with perfecting this new piece of equipment to help people all around the world. I became on a mission.

I was on a mission from God; I had to get to the bottom of it and figure this out.

Peter continued to use the equipment, and he refined and improved it, enjoying all the benefits improved health and mobility had to offer.

> After using this machine for a while, my fitness level improved so much that people around town thought I was using some type of illegal drug. People half my age couldn't keep up with me. They'd ask, "Hey Peter, what kind of drugs are you taking? Whatever it is, I'm sure it's not legal, but we need to know about it." I told them I wasn't taking any drugs, but I'm not sure they believed me.
>
> A group of older men accused me of the same thing too. Again, I told them I wasn't on any drugs but had developed a piece of equipment that helped me heal from some injuries and get in a good workout in very little time. They didn't believe me either, so I invited them to my house to try it.
>
> To my delight, five older men took me up on my offer. The youngest one was 60 years old. They were all in their 60s and early 70s. They came over three to five times a week to use the equipment.

After a few weeks of using the equipment, each of the men started experiencing a myriad of benefits, such as improved fitness, elevated libidos, and testosterone levels of a typical 40-year-old. "That's when I realized that we were providing a huge uptake to the endocrine system without using any kind of steroids or drugs. It was all natural. And that's when I started focusing on perfecting and promoting the technology 24/7."

Peter continued to refine and improve the equipment until it was ready for market. As of this writing, he is still going strong at 73 years of age, telling me he has no plans to slow down and has achieved true happiness in life by helping others solve health problems and achieve optimal performance using the equipment he developed—the Vasper System.

If you want to be happy for five minutes, take a nap. If you want to be happy for two weeks, take a vacation. If you want to be happy from time to time, have a drink or do whatever else gives you pleasure. But if you want continuous ramifications in life, continuous happiness, keep creating positive differences in the lives of others.

How the Vasper System Can Optimize Your Physical Health in Just 21 Minutes

As Peter notes, exercise is the most powerful thing you can do for your health. Exercise produces anabolic hormones, especially when you exercise at high intensity. Those hormones, along with other exercise benefits, improve vitality, help your body heal from injuries, increase energy, elevate performance, and more.

But many successful business owners or high-income earners can't complete the high-intensity exercise programs required to achieve those benefits, and others. Between their busy schedules, the natural decline in base-level hormones, and elevated stress levels, business owners often can't carve out the time or withstand the intensity required to achieve all the benefits high-intensity training provides.

That's where Peter and the Vasper exercise system come in. Vasper enables anyone regardless of age or fitness level to mimic the physiology of an intensive workout and experience the same benefits without the same wear and tear or time. It delivers this benefit through a highly effective, safe, sustainable, low-impact, 21-minute workout.

The results? Using Vasper for just 21 minutes has been shown to

- increase anabolic hormone levels,
- reduce stress hormones, specifically nighttime cortisol,
- create a major improvement to sleep quality,
- build lean muscle,
- increase energy levels,
- increase metabolism function,
- increase focus and motivation,

- expedite recovery after injury,
- improve cognitive health and neurological function,
- decrease inflammation,
- and more.

Like everything I do and like with every expert who makes it onto my team, I personally vetted both Peter and Vasper and reviewed the science behind how it works. Vasper is based on three scientifically proven principles—compression technology, liquid cooling, and interval training. The synergy between these three elements creates the effect users experience.

Vasper's compression technology involves placing compression cuffs on the arm and leg muscles while exercising at a low intensity. This has been scientifically shown to create the physiological effect of high-intensity exercise. Compression cuffs worn on the arms and legs safely compress the muscle to quickly build up lactic acid, mimicking the physiology of an intense workout that would typically take extensive time and effort. Compression builds metabolite concentration quickly and activates fast-twitch muscle fibers. This triggers a systemic recovery response, including the natural release of anabolic hormones such as testosterone.

Vasper's liquid cooling technology helps keep your body temperature cool while you work out, which causes several benefits. Specifically, when your body temperature rises, blood vessels near the surface of the skin dilate. That increases blood flow and oxygen to your skin, leaving less for the muscles. As blood leaves your muscles, lactic acid begins to build up in your muscles and your body hits a wall and fatigues. Staying cool during exercise allows blood oxygen levels to remain high throughout the body, which makes exercising much more efficient and pleasant. In fact, sweating is also dramatically reduced or completely eliminated, making a Vasper possible even in the middle of a workday. In fact, most Vasper users report no muscle soreness following their session. Vasper is designed to be a moderate, low-impact, nondamaging exercise session that still delivers the benefits of an intensive workout.

Its users have reported tremendous benefits, and all from simple 21-minute workouts. For example, Dan Sullivan, the cofounder of the executive coaching program Strategic Coach, reports that "Over the first 15 months of using Vasper more than 3x weekly, I've gained 6 pounds of muscle, lost 14 pounds of fat, increased my testosterone score from 379 to 697, and have enjoyed the most relaxed, energized, creative, and productive period of my life. All of this at age 72. My success story has so far persuaded 100+ other Strategic Coach entrepreneurs to purchase their own Vasper."

Over the 21-minute workout, Vasper puts you through an interval training circuit that, combined with compression and liquid cooling, helps you get all the benefits of long, high-intensity, high-impact workouts on one piece of equipment in the comfort of your own home or office.

Or if you prefer to get out of the house or office for your 21-minute workout, you could visit one of several locations around the country. Having Peter on my cohesive team of specialists opens the door to a number of possibilities for you to use Vasper to optimize your body and mind. Here is more about just some of the ways the Vasper System can help you turn back the clock.

The Negative Side Effects of Exercising the Traditional Way

Nobody will suggest that exercise is bad for you. "Exercise is the best form of medicine you can have," Peter says. "But most people do not exercise every day because of the side effects. You sweat. You cause damage to your muscles, cartilage, and ligaments. You become sore. And you need time to recover from exercise."

Peter shared with me that people tend to end up doing one of two extremes when it comes to exercise, in part because of the side effects. "Some people end up doing very light exercise to avoid side effects. While there's nothing wrong with that, walking is not exercise—at least not in the sense of triggering significant physiological improvements like what more high-intensity workouts trigger."

On the other side of the extreme, people end up overtraining. They try to get the benefits of doing true high-intensity workouts multiple times a week but end up overdoing it:

> Some people do workout programs like CrossFit, Insanity, or P90X, and end up overtraining. Professional athletes do too. Not only can this cause injuries but your body needs hormones to heal from such high-intensity workouts, so your body won't benefit from all the hormones you produce from the workout because it needs so much of them just to recover from overtraining.

The compression, circulation, and cooling technologies built into the Vasper System make it so you generate all the same hormonal responses as those high-intensity workouts but don't develop the side effects that use up so many of those hormones to recover.

Sleep Soundly, Cut the Need for Caffeine, Improve Mental Clarity, and More

Imagine not needing caffeine to wake up or function past the 3:00 p.m. lull. That's one of the most reported benefits of using the Vasper System, says Peter.

> The most reported benefit of Vasper—by far—is a tremendous increase in the quality of sleep. From athletes to type-A businesspeople, the quality of their sleep quickly improves. Because a good night's sleep has so many benefits, we also offer clients a sleep protocol that helps improve sleep even further. Our clients regularly report having amazing sleep and performing at a much higher level.
>
> Many of our clients are used to making coffee first thing in the morning just to start their day. Some even use a smart coffee maker to automatically brew coffee 10 minutes before their alarm goes off so they don't have to wait for it to brew. After working with the Vasper System for as little as two weeks, everyone from

businesspeople to athletes to elite military unit members report not even needing caffeine anymore because of the natural boost they got in energy levels from the increased hormone production.

The Vasper System is used by people from 10 years old to 97. It has been determined to be safe in a study of adults conducted by the company, too.[3] And although many of the success stories from patients are anecdotal, they are nonetheless impressive in how they've been able to help patients and their families make tremendous positive improvements in their lives.

For example, one Vasper System client came to Peter after being practically bedridden with fibromyalgia for 14 years. Peter recounts:

> She needed a wheelchair to get around. Her husband had to basically carry her and place her into the Vasper System. At the beginning of the session, we needed to help her do the exercises. We had to help her move her arms and legs. She wasn't able to move on her own. During the session, she started to be able to do more on her own and, by the end, she felt great. Not only that but she stood up off the chair and walked for the first time in years, with tears forming in her eyes.

These are just some of the stories Peter has collected over the years from users who were able to achieve incredible and measurable improvements in their lives. And it all comes from the impact of the Vasper System technology on our bodies.

---

3   Jeff Gladden et al., "Pilot Safety Study: The Use of Vasper[TM], a Novel Blood Flow Restriction Exercise in Healthy Adults," Journal of Exercise Physiology Online 19, no. 2 (April 2016): 99+, https://go.gale.com/ps/i.do?p=AONE&u=mlin_oweb&id=GA-LEA462045144&v=2.1&it=r&sid=googleScholar&asid=70a06459&password=NostimonH-mar&ugroup=outside

Achieve Better Hormonal and Emotional Balance

"Our optimal hormonal balance is what you see in a child," says Peter. He notes:

> As we age or want to improve performance and our hormone levels change, traditional medicine calls for people to inject hormones into our bodies to supplement the decline. We saw a lot of this in professional sports, with athletes using human growth hormone to come back from injury or increase performance. For example, growth hormone helps improve visual acuity. So baseball players have taken it to see the baseball better, which makes it much easier to hit.

While understandable, Peter notes that injecting supplements into our system is not without its side effects.

> Many of those people have never been informed of the side effects of injecting hormones into your body from the outside. In the case of human growth hormone, for example, if you inject growth hormone, you flood your brain with synthetic growth hormone—even "bioidentical" growth hormone. That's a marketing term. The effect of injecting it into your body is the same—it floods your brain with growth hormone.
>
> If you flood your brain with growth hormone from the outside, your pituitary gland will learn that it doesn't need to make as much growth hormone anymore and slow down. If you inject enough into your body, it will learn that it doesn't need to make *any* growth hormone and stop completely.
>
> The effects of your pituitary gland slowing down production cascade from there, including a downstream anabolic effect, including some people whose bodies stop naturally producing testosterone and needing steroids to make testosterone.

We see a lot of growth hormone supplementation in children who are not growing as expected. Boosting their human growth hormone helps offset their lack of natural production and causes them to grow. But unnatural supplementation can cause your hormonal balance to go "out the window," Peter says. "When your hormones are out of balance, your mental and emotional balance also goes out the window. This can cause people to act aggressively and suffer from significant mental health challenges. I believe that the best pharmacy is inside your own body."

After one client's parents heard about Vasper System's natural way to boost growth hormone production, they decided to try the Vasper regime instead of growth hormone supplementation for their 10-year-old who wasn't growing.

> This 10-year-old boy had been growing at a rate of about a half a millimeter per month. Not wanting to inject him with hormones, his parents looked for answers. It just so happened that the San Jose *Mercury* did a story about us at the time that the parents read. In the article, it mentions how the Vasper System causes the body to release extra doses of natural growth hormones.[4]
>
> The parents decided to try putting him on Vasper before injecting him with hormones, and it worked. After one month, he grew around eight or nine millimeters. We were all elated at how this one aspect of the Vasper System technology could make such a big difference for this young boy.
>
> Even the child's physicians were surprised. One was skeptical.
>
> The child's pediatric endocrinologist was very skeptical, asking us how we knew the child didn't just happen to have entered a growth spurt. Truthfully, it was possible. Even if we hadn't put him on a Vasper System regime, he could have just had a growth

---

4   Chris O'Brien, "Is Vasper Really the Exercise of the Future?," *The Mercury News*, February 2, 2012, https://www.mercurynews.com/2012/02/02/obrien-is-vasper-really-the-exercise-of-the-future/.

spurt. I didn't want to get into an argument with the guy, so I just politely told him he could be right.

About six months later, however, a car accident would give us all the data we would need to know who was right. His sister was severely injured in the car accident and required 24/7 attention to heal, so nobody could bring the boy for his Vasper sessions. He had to stop. As soon as he did, his growth rate fell down to where it was when he started. Once she healed and he was able to restart his Vasper sessions, his growth rate came up again.

It is well known that exercise can help achieve mental clarity, too, and everyone from high achievers to autistic teenagers has reported these benefits when using the Vasper System.

One of our early investors had a 14-year-old son on the autism spectrum. His doctors managed some of the impact of the autism using a series of drugs. When his father first brought the boy in, he was lethargic. It was impossible to have a normal conversation with him.

His father wanted him to try a few sessions on the Vasper System to see what impact it could have on the boy. At first, the boy refused. It took me two days to convince him to get on the machine. But on the second day, he agreed to try it. When he got off, he had a completely different energy. The first thing he did was hug me and tell me this was the first time he could remember his brain "not going 100 miles an hour."

To assess the effect of the Vasper System on your natural hormones, Vasper tested testosterone levels in five professional baseball players, who each used the Vasper System eight times over two weeks. Of the baseball players, four out of the five saw an increase in free testosterone levels, with an average increase of 132 percent. Although this particular study focused on a small group, the many positive impacts of high-intensity interval training, or HIIT, are well known. And with the Vasper System helping create the equivalent of a two-hour HIIT workout in about 20 minutes, it is easy to see why so many clients are experiencing such positive results using the Vasper System.

Keys to Chapter

- Like other areas of specialty, when a client expresses a desire to improve a certain area of their life, I present them with options through my extended network. If they decide to move forward with one of the solutions, they work directly with those providers. I make nothing from making these introductions, but it's a core part of my DiNuzzo Middle-Market Family Office mission and culture of serving clients' needs and wants.

- Common requests by successful business owners involve improving physical fitness, energy levels, and quality of life. And one of the solutions I've helped connect clients to is the Vasper System, which was created by physiology expert and human performance specialist Peter Wasowski. I have also purchased and personally use the Vasper System myself, with great results.

- As we get older, a number of things start happening in our bodies, including a decline in our natural production of hormones, such as testosterone, estrogen, growth hormone, and even melatonin. This is important because hormones are our bodies' natural support systems for many of our organs and systems. One of the most powerful tools we have to improve our natural body function is exercise.

- One problem many successful middle-market business owners experience when exercising is that they can't complete the high-intensity exercise programs required to achieve optimal fitness and hormone levels. Another problem is that typical high-intensity exercise comes with significant negative side effects, such as muscle soreness, sweat, and cartilage damage.

- That's where Peter and the Vasper exercise system come in. Vasper enables anyone regardless of age or fitness level to mimic the physiology of an intensive workout and experience the same benefits without the same wear and tear or time. It delivers this benefit through a highly effective, safe, sustainable, low-impact 21-minute workout, and without all the negative side effects of typical high-intensity exercise programs. Vasper has been shown to increase anabolic hormone levels, reduce stress hormones, improve sleep quality, build lean muscles, increase energy levels, and more.

Chapter 18

Anti-Aging Biohacking to Turn Back the Clock

I probably don't have to tell you about all the changes that happen to us as we age. From wrinkles to pain, as the years go by, how we look and feel changes over time. But we don't have to just accept that we will begin to look and feel old as the calendar turns thanks to one of many biohacking techniques available to us.

If you've already received all the benefits of executive medicine, concierge medicine, and efficient fitness, Amy Gardner and her colleagues at LightStim can help. Using various light therapy solutions, LightStim can help you begin to turn back the clock on how you look and feel. You don't need to spend a lot of time using LightStim's solutions either. In just 20 minutes, you can begin experiencing several anti-aging and pain reduction benefits.

After working with hundreds of successful middle-market business owners and thousands of wealthy families since 1989, I've learned that successful people don't just want to be successful in business. They want to look and feel successful too. However, they become so busy building their business and family that they can often let their personal wellness suffer.

I feel the same way, too, and that's why I work closely with Amy and the team at LightStim to help my clients use their technology to look and feel better. But I don't just use LightStim to help my clients. I use it as well. I own their LightStim LED Bed, which you will hear about momentarily, and I have personally experienced several benefits from it, including increased energy, reduced inflammation, faster post-workout recovery, optimized blood pressure, and reduced stress. Although my experience is anecdotal, the benefits of LightStim's biohacking technology are much more than anecdotal, as you'll read below.

How LightStim and Light Therapy and Personal Health Expert Amy Gardner Help Change the Lives of Clients, Their Families, and Their Businesses

Amy Gardner is the Director of Education at LightStim, a company with a range of solutions that deliver light energy to your body similar to how plants absorb light energy from the sun. Each LightStim device uses different wavelengths, or colors of light, to help patients begin to look and feel better.

Their LightStim for Wrinkles device uses various wavelengths of amber, red, and infrared light to reduce fine lines and wrinkles for a more youthful appearance. LightStim for Acne uses blue light to destroy acne-causing bacteria and red light to help soothe and calm the skin. This helps clear existing breakouts in order to give you visibly improved, healthy-looking skin. LightStim for Pain emits four different wavelengths of red and infrared light energy that reduce pain and increase local blood circulation. Increased circulation accelerates your body's recovery process, relaxes muscles, and can relieve minor muscle and joint pain and stiffness. This combination of wavelengths is what's used in their full body device—the LightStim LED Bed. The Bed offers a noninvasive, soothing, and gentle treatment that sets in motion the body's inherent pain-relieving process. LED light therapy is also known as red light therapy, low-level light therapy, or photobiomodulation.

LightStim's solutions are not just backed by anecdotal stories either. LightStim for Wrinkles is cleared by the FDA for the treatment of fine lines and wrinkles, LightStim for Acne is FDA cleared to treat mild to moderate acne, and LightStim for Pain (including the LightStim LED Bed) is FDA cleared for several applications, including the temporary relief of muscle, joint, and arthritic pain as well as the increase of local blood circulation.

About Light Therapy

Light therapy is a rapidly growing field in which Amy has immersed herself for over 12 years. She shared the following with me on the subject of light therapy in general. As such, her comments below are not intended to represent LightStim claims.

"It's hard to believe that something so gentle, soothing, and seemingly simple could possibly have so many profound effects on health and appearance, but hundreds of studies and thousands of papers over approximately the past 50 years have shown this to be the case. Low-level light therapy is a relaxing, noninvasive treatment that utilizes low levels of light which are absorbed by cells and tissues. This absorbed energy triggers multiple cellular processes involved in healing and repair," Amy explains. "We have molecules in our cells that absorb light, or electromagnetic energy. It's not something we think about, but we're all familiar with biological processes that are directly affected by the body's absorption of light. For example, we spend a little time in the sun and our bodies begin to synthesize vitamin D. Daylight floods the room and we're suddenly wide awake because of a reduction in our melatonin, whether we want to be or not. These are just a couple of examples of photobiochemical events, so it's not really a leap to consider that there are many others."

Amy continues, "As we age, our cells become damaged from overall wear and tear along with ongoing environmental assaults like UV radiation, pollution, poor diet, and perhaps drinking too much alcohol. All of these things generate free radicals or "unbalanced" molecules that set off a chain reaction which contributes to chronic inflammation and ultimately cell damage. Ongoing and unmanaged stress can also influence what goes on at a cellular level in terms of health and longevity," she says. "A little stress is good for us and can even trigger protective mechanisms, but too much or the wrong kind of stress is quite another matter."

"Studies show that when you provide light energy to the cells it gets converted to cellular energy used for repair, regeneration, and beneficial signaling," says Amy. "Light therapy essentially provides critical resources that promote more youthful and productive cellular behavior."

From Ancient Wisdom to Modern Technology

The benefits of sunlight have been understood for thousands of years. Hippocrates was a big proponent, and Olympian athletes were actually required to sunbathe. In the 1800s to early 1900s solariums became popular throughout Europe. Patients visited these medical facilities for "heliotherapy"—to soak up the sun as treatment for a variety of conditions of the joints and skin, as well as tuberculosis.

Amy explains, "The major downside to natural sunlight, of course, is UV. Ultraviolet radiation does have benefits and is sometimes used to treat certain conditions like psoriasis, but it can also damage DNA. Fortunately, modern technology allows us to utilize only proven beneficial wavelengths of light. In essence, we've learned to extract what is healing about sunlight, thereby eliminating concern over negative side effects associated with UV exposure."

Observed Benefits of Light Therapy

As evidence on the benefits of light therapy grows, so does interest among those who seek a proactive and preventive approach to health and well-being. Here's what Amy had to say about some of the benefits:

Increased Cellular Energy

Studies indicate that light therapy can increase production of the body's cellular fuel, adenosine triphosphate (ATP). This is quite significant because most biological processes are ATP-dependent, meaning that cells require energy for things like tissue repair, immune function, elimination of waste, and cell signaling. If there's not enough energy at the level of the cell, entire systems can fail, leading to degeneration and disease.

The body has mechanisms to support growth, maintenance, repair, and protection, but it needs fuel to power these processes. In this sense, the body is like a well-designed automobile—it may be in great shape mechanistically, but without fuel, it simply can't do what it was built to do.

ATP is particularly important as we age because studies have shown a marked decline in our ability to produce it after the age of 18.

Beneficial Gene Expression

As we know, we each have a genetic code or DNA that is inherited from our parents. While we can't change this coding, we do have some influence over how our genes are expressed. In other words, certain habits or practices can sort of "turn up" or "turn down" how much or how little of a gene product (like a protein) our bodies produce. This is very important because proteins do most of the work in the cells and are essential for the structure, function, and regulation of the body's tissues and organs.

Light therapy has been shown to affect gene expression in a beneficial way. In fact, it's often referred to as "the great regulator" by many researchers because it can help regulate gene expression for the better, making adjustments to suit the circumstances. For example, it may temporarily upregulate inflammatory cytokines (small proteins associated with inflammation) in order to repair a wound, but under different circumstances, it may downregulate those cytokines to alleviate chronic low-grade inflammation that's out of control and potentially damaging.

Reduced Inflammation

Over the past 20 years or so, our growing understanding of the effects of inflammation has radically changed our prevention strategies as well as our responses when things go awry. It's now widely acknowledged that chronic low-grade inflammation plays a role in most disease processes as well as the aging process in general.

Unlike redness and swelling that you may see on the surface of the skin (known as acute inflammation) chronic low-grade inflammation is internal, and therefore, unseen and undetected. It can be systemic and often manifests in response to some of the lifestyle and environmental triggers we talked about earlier. One of the major benefits of light therapy as demonstrated in studies is its ability to regulate inflammation, essentially "resetting" our biological landscape from inflammatory to noninflammatory.

Enhancing Circulation and Lowering Blood Pressure

As I've mentioned, there's a lot of beneficial cell signaling that goes on with light therapy. Some of this can be attributed to nitric oxide. Like ATP, nitric oxide, or NO, is a compound naturally produced by the body. Also, like ATP, the older we get the less nitric oxide we produce, and what we do produce can become trapped in cells where it can inhibit ATP production.

Nitric oxide plays a critical role in many areas of general health including vasodilation, immune function, and neurotransmission. Its impact is so profound that in 1998 three scientists won the Nobel Prize for identifying its many benefits, and it was dubbed "the miracle molecule."

Light therapy has been shown to release trapped nitric oxide from the cells allowing ATP production to resume normally. As nitric oxide is released, it becomes available to the body for important signaling functions including vasodilation (dilation of blood vessels). Nitric oxide signals blood vessels to relax and expand thereby relieving high blood pressure or hypertension. There is great potential here, especially given that one out of every three adults in the U.S. suffers from high blood pressure, which can lead to heart attacks and strokes.

Improving Performance and Recovery

I know I've talked a lot about aging and illness, but light therapy also offers amazing benefits for anyone interested in optimizing their physical performance. It is now widely used by fitness buffs, sports enthusiasts, and professional athletes. The reason is simple: muscle tissue is rich in mitochondria, the cellular organelles where ATP is produced. Mitochondria are essentially the body's tiny power plants. They are also home to the molecules where most red and infrared light gets absorbed. So a high concentration of mitochondria results in a high concentration of cellular energy generated by absorbed light. This translates to increased stamina, less exercise-induced cell damage, and improved recovery.

Mindfulness and Stress Management: A Holistic Approach

One of the fastest-growing areas of interest and research on light therapy has to do with its effects on the brain. Amy shared how she uses light therapy to enhance the effects she receives from mindfulness.

Amy started practicing mindfulness out of necessity. Like many, she began to see the effects of ongoing stress on her health as well as her quality of life. As she began working on stress reduction, she learned about mindfulness and how so few of us are present in the moment, paying attention to ourselves and our surroundings without judgment.

My experience with mindfulness and meditation is one that is shared globally and on a massive level. Societal pressures, work ethic, and desire to "do better" in every area of life can foster habits that become ingrained in our brains and acted upon in a "mind-*less*" way. When I began to do some research and realized that I actually had the power to redirect thoughts and behaviors for better health and quality of life, I decided to enroll in an eight-week class on Mindfulness-Based Stress Reduction (MBSR), a program developed at the University of Massachusetts Medical Center about 40 years ago. You might say that the folks at UMass were among the earliest western pioneers of mindfulness. Since that time, I've participated in many classes and retreats, all invaluable. There are now endless programs and techniques for developing mindfulness. The key is in finding one that's a fit for you.

Paying attention in the present moment without judgment sounds pretty easy, but it's actually an extraordinarily difficult thing to do. Research from Harvard shows that the mind wanders approximately 47 percent of the time, and we mindlessly judge most everything—especially our own behavior. However, if we train ourselves to develop awareness, the benefits are immeasurable. It can bring more peace, improve the quality of our relationships, and help us to be more effective and productive at work. Being where you are as opposed to drifting also allows you to make the most of life's experiences because you show up in a very different way to participate in them. Nobody wants to wake up one day and say, "I wish I'd participated more in life."

The connection with light therapy has to do with the growth, reorganization, and improved function of neurons in the brain. Both mindfulness and light therapy have been shown in studies to help facilitate these things. I'm a huge believer in doing things with a common purpose that support each other, and in my opinion, these two practices do. I also strongly believe in a holistic approach. If we want to maintain health and optimize our performance, we need to attend to the mind as well as the body. There is just no denying that biochemistry connects everything.

Biohacking Technology as an Asset

I asked Amy how light therapy could add value to our clients' lives, and here's what she had to say:

"All that we learn about light therapy indicates that it gently intervenes to help the body do what it already knows how to do but has become sluggish at over time. When we improve the body's overall performance, we look better, feel better, are more creative, and have more confidence and positivity—all things that are essential for both business and personal success."

Keys to Chapter

- Some of my clients request referrals to specialists who can help them with anti-aging, pain reduction, and skincare solutions. One of the best introductions I can make for those concerns is to Amy Gardner and her colleagues at LightStim. I work closely with Amy and the team at LightStim to help my clients use their technology to look and feel better. I also personally own one of their premier solutions and have experienced several benefits.

- LightStim produces a range of solutions that deliver light energy to your body similar to how plants absorb light energy from the sun. Each LightStim device uses different wavelengths, or colors of light, to help patients begin to look and feel better.

- For example, their LightStim for Wrinkles device uses various wavelengths of amber, red, and infrared light to reduce fine lines and wrinkles for a more youthful appearance. LightStim for Acne uses blue light to destroy acne-causing bacteria and red light to help soothe and calm the skin. LightStim for Pain emits four different wavelengths of red and infrared light energy that reduce pain and increase local blood circulation. The LightStim LED Bed uses the same combination of four wavelengths to offer a noninvasive, soothing, and gentle treatment that sets in motion the entire body's inherent pain-relieving process.

- LightStim's solutions have received various clearances from the FDA for several applications, including for the treatment of fine lines and wrinkles, the treatment of mild or moderate acne, temporary relief of muscle, joint, and arthritic pain, and the increase of local blood circulation.

- As evidence on the benefits of light therapy grows, so does interest among those who seek a proactive and preventive approach to health and well-being. Recognized benefits include increased cellular energy, beneficial gene expression, reduced inflammation, enhanced circulation, lowered blood pressure, improved performance and recovery, and stress management.

PART 5:

———

Experiencing the DiNuzzo Middle-Market Family Office Way

———

Chapter 19

How Engaging the DiNuzzo Middle-Market Family Office Can Be a Life-Changing Event *for You*

When new clients come to my DiNuzzo Middle-Market Family Office™, they often have several things in common. They are successful. They are high achievers. They work hard. They know how to sacrifice. They put other people before themselves, including both family members and employees. They are givers. They want to leave the world a better place than they found it—for their families, employees, and communities.

But there is also something missing. They don't always sleep well. Some have high stress levels. A number are often carrying a little (or a lot) too much weight, and their health is struggling in many ways. Quite a few haven't taken a true vacation in *years*, always glued to their computers or phones no matter where in the world they find themselves. Many of them are worried about risk. They'll often tell you they pay too much in taxes. It's common for many of them that their cash flow is too low or inconsistent. For a solid majority of them, they spend way too much time working *in* their business and not nearly enough time working *on* their business. The list goes on. Just about every successful middle-market business owner or wealthy family suffers from some combination of those issues, and others.

Identifying and resolving those issues while optimizing the parts of your life that are going well is how engaging my DMMFO can be a life-changing event for you.

Why I Built My DiNuzzo Middle-Market Family Office™

One of the most frequently asked questions I receive from my DMMFO clients involves why I built my DMMFO. After building a successful wealth management firm and helping my wealth management clients become so successful, why change anything? Why build an entirely new business? Why put myself through the process of scouring the country (and sometimes beyond …) to identify the best-of-the-best experts in a subject matter no Wealth Manager even cares about, let alone coordinates *pro bono* for clients? What fix something that wasn't broken?

Frankly, my intent in 1989 was not to develop the first and only true family office level of service for successful middle-market business owners. My initial intent was to provide the best possible service for my Wealth Management clients. But the combination of the natural market factors that made my DMMFO possible and the continued growth that I helped my Wealth Management clients achieve made building my DMMFO a natural next step for me.

Frankly, over time my wealth management clients needed more help than was available to them as their wealth grew. I didn't walk in and open the doors to my DMMFO one day as a new business. It evolved over time from my wealth management firm. After several years in business, I helped grow my clients' wealth to the point that many of them became underserved by other professionals, so I started looking for more specialized and experienced professionals to help them, some of whom also advised Single Family Offices. As more time passed, I began to question why no viable options existed for middle-market business owners like my clients that gave them the same level of service as Single Family Offices. I learned that the biggest issue was not the need—successful middle-market business owners had the same needs as the ultra-wealthy, just not the same volume. I learned that the biggest problem was the model of the existing options—they were too expensive.

So as more and more of my clients truly needed the level of service once only available to the ultra-wealthy through Single Family Offices, I committed to solving the problems that plagued the industry in the first place and left them as a forgotten, underserved demographic. And, between restructuring fees and being able to work completely virtually, I was finally able to do what so many other professionals either could not or would not do: bring a Single Family Office level of care to successful middle-market business owners and wealthy families. My DMMFO has been a work-in-progress since 1989, constantly evolving as a natural extension of my wealth management firm as my clients' needs grew over time. It was a natural evolution.

I built my DMMFO with one goal in mind: to help improve the lives of the forgotten demographic—successful middle-market business owners and wealthy families. I built it to bring optimization and peace of mind to every area of your life. I built it so you feel as successful on the inside as you appear to others on the outside. That's because I believe that true success only comes when you feel successful on the inside and out. It requires you to be at peace at work, at home, and within yourself.

Unlike professionals who operate at lower levels of the Private Wealth Hierarchy, which I discussed earlier, I built my DMMFO to help you achieve that true level of success in all areas of your life. That's why I have as many health and wellness experts on my cohesive team of specialists or in my extended network as I do CPAs and attorneys. That's why I treat your body and mind with the same level of care and concern as I treat your business and bank accounts. That's why my DMMFO core team includes experts on every area of your life.

Yes, I have the best-of-the-best experts to help you improve your businesses, grow your wealth, manage risk, reduce tax obligations, optimize your estate plan, and more. Those outcomes are important. But I want to make an even bigger impact on your life. I want you to live the life you deserve. That means

- Achieving a higher entity value
- Having clear succession and estate plans
- Protecting wealth for generations
- Spending more quality time with people you love
- Maximizing your physical and mental wellness
- Taking care of your spouse, partner, children, grandchildren, and other family members as well as possible
- Living your life how you want to, when you want to, the way you deserve
- Reducing taxes
- Improving business operations
- Increasing and stabilizing cash flows
- Helping you live the life you want
- Increasing your base level physical and mental health
- Reducing stress
- Improving sleep
- Achieving your optimal health and lifestyle
- Maximizing your body and your mind
- Making my DMMFO a profit center for you
- And more

When you get to your level of success, small but sophisticated changes can create a significant positive impact on your balance sheet. It's not uncommon for me to save clients at your level hundreds of thousands of dollars a year in tax obligations, for example. Those results are important. My clients appreciate all the financial benefits they achieve through my DMMFO.

But what really moves the needle for my clients are the lifestyle results they experience along the way. Stress melts away. Energy levels skyrocket. They sleep well for the first time in a long time. They achieve a work-life balance they never thought possible. They can even live longer, healthier lives.

And, unlike other professionals, my clients only pay for the value they receive. If they are not interested in healthcare, they don't use or pay for those services. If they have professionals in place who are serving them well, my team and I work closely with them to supplement and complement them. We don't come in and try to replace people who are serving you well.

Your services and benefits are completely customized to your unique goals and needs. We don't force anything on you. And, with everything we do, we present you with options, along with the pros and cons to each, and help *you* make a decision about which option you choose, if any.

And that's how my DMMFO model can provide a life-changing experience for you.

Keys to Chapter

- I built my DiNuzzo Middle-Market Family Office with one goal in mind: to help improve the lives of the forgotten demographic—successful middle-market business owners and wealthy families.

- When you get to your level of success, small but sophisticated changes can create a significant positive impact on your balance sheet. It's not uncommon for me to save clients at your level hundreds of thousands of dollars a year in tax obligations, for example. But that's just the beginning of the benefits my clients can experience.

- Unlike professionals who operate at lower levels of the Private Wealth Hierarchy, I built my DMMFO to help you achieve that true level of success in all areas of your life. That's why I have as many health and wellness experts on my cohesive team of specialists or in my extended network as I do CPAs and attorneys. That's why I treat your body and mind with the same level of care and concern as I treat your business and bank accounts. That's why my DMMFO core team includes experts on every area of your life.

- And unlike other professionals, my clients only pay for the value they receive. If they are not interested in healthcare, they don't use or pay for those services. If they have professionals in place who are serving them well, my team and I work closely with them to supplement and complement them. We don't come in and try to replace people who are serving you well.
- My DMMFO provides life-changing experiences for our clients because everything we do is customized for my clients' unique needs and desires.

Chapter 20

How to Tell Whether the DiNuzzo Middle-Market Family Office is the Right Choice for You

L et me make one thing clear from the start. I've seen how much of an impact my DiNuzzo Middle-Market Family Office™ can make on successful middle-market business owners and wealthy families. Between business, financial, personal, and philanthropic goals, there's no part of your life that my DMMFO can't help you improve.

Moreover, because I structured my DMMFO model in such a value-focused way that it can become an actual profit center for you and your business, I've made the financial considerations as favorable as possible to my clients.

That said, if you're content and confident that you and your team have the pieces in place to optimize your life in all the ways I discussed in this book, my DMMFO might not be for you. It's not for everyone. It's not a *requirement*.

But if your business or life is complex, meaning that you require more than just plain vanilla answers in your world, my DMMFO might be a consideration for you.

If you just want to make sure you are optimizing your business and financial world and don't know if you are, my DMMFO might be a consideration for you.

And, in my experience, if you don't know whether you are optimizing your business and financial world, the odds are that you are not. To know that you are, you need to know several things with complete certainty. For example, you need to know that your professionals

- truly have your best interests at heart and are not "pretenders" or salespeople disguised as professionals.
- do not *just* have your interests at heart but are truly the best-of-the-best in their fields with both the experience and sophistication to identify nuances that impact people in your position.
- have asked you all the right questions to give you custom plans and high-impact solutions that optimize both the human and technical concerns involved.
- work seamlessly together to ensure that all pieces of your plans will function as desired. For example, that means all property is properly titled to match trusts and insurance policies.

And these are just the big-picture things you need to know to understand whether your business and financial world is optimized. For example, if your professionals didn't go through a process like the discovery process I described in this book, your world is likely not optimized. And if they didn't present you with multiple options for achieving each of your goals and explain the pros and cons for each option to allow you to make an informed decision, your world is likely not optimized.

In the end, if you are unsure, the answer is almost always that your business and financial world is *not* optimized. Even then, to be clear, my DMMFO is not a *requirement* for all middle-market business owners and wealthy families. In fact, it's not a fit for all middle-market business owners and wealthy families.

In other words, this is not something you must do, but it *is* something you might want to seriously consider if you are a middle-market business owner who

- earns $1 million or more per year,
- owns a business generating $10 million or more in revenue per year,
- has a net worth of at least $10 million, or
- is quickly approaching one or more of those three benchmarks.

That's because, for me to be able to make engaging my DMMFO a truly life-changing event for you, you need to have a commensurate level of complexity in your business and personal life and a large enough financial world that single moves can generate hundreds of thousands of dollars of value for you, or more.

You have to have assets to work with as well. If you have nothing, and that's an extreme, I know, my DMMFO will do nothing for you. If you don't have assets to protect, you don't have taxes to pay. You don't have much to worry about in terms of sophisticated asset protection, succession planning, estate planning, or financial planning.

But if you do have assets and complexity, the next question becomes whether your professionals are truly world-class and fully integrated. Ask yourself whether everything and everyone is working together on your behalf. Did they coordinate to effectuate the plans you have in place or has everything been piecemeal with you being the only common thread? It's one person doing one thing and another person doing another, with every professional only concerning themselves with their particular expertise.

If these issues cause you some pause, my DMMFO might be able to help you in every area of your life. My team and I could help optimize your business, helping you go from working *in* your business to *on* your business. We could help you grow revenue, reduce expenses, save taxes, improve cash flow, and increase entity value. We could help you put together and execute a sophisticated succession or exit plan. We could help you optimize your estate plan, investments, and even your personal health.

In most cases, people don't have all of these pieces of their life optimized. They have a few pieces in place but not all. They have some business pieces and some financial pieces, but their health is suffering. Or their business and health are in good places, but their family is struggling. Engaging my DMMFO helps ensure every part of your life that is important to you is optimized to your goals.

In the end, if all these things are not happening in your life, my DMMFO might very well be the right answer for you. It's built to provide you with the exact levels of service that the wealthiest families in the world achieve using the Single Family Office model. These extremely wealthy families build their own private Single Family Office for the same reasons that my DMMFO could be a life-changing event for you. They have complexity. They have assets. They have big goals. So they hire the best-of-the-best experts to optimize their life.

We do the same using a different compensation model that makes it work for middle-market business owners and wealthy families.

If that sounds like an improvement to what you are currently experiencing, my DMMFO might be something worth considering.

 ## Keys to Chapter

- If you're content and confident that you and your team have the pieces in place to optimize your business, financial, and personal life in all the ways I discussed in this book, my DiNuzzo Middle-Market Family Office might not be for you. It's not for everyone. It's not a *requirement*. But …

- … if your business or life is complex, meaning that you require more than just plain vanilla answers in your world, my DMMFO might be a consideration for you.

- In my experience, if you don't know whether you are optimizing your business and financial world, the odds are that you are not. And if you are a middle-market business owner who (1) earns $1 million or more per year, (2) owns a business generating $10 million or more in revenue per year, (3) has a net worth of at least $10 million, or (4) is quickly approaching one or more of those three benchmarks, my DMMFO might be a good fit for you.

- In most cases, people don't have all of these pieces of their life optimized. They have a few pieces in place but not all. They have some business pieces and some financial pieces, but their health is suffering. Or their business and health are in good places, but their family is struggling. Engaging my DMMFO helps ensure every part of your life that is important to you is optimized to your goals.
- My DMMFO is built to provide you with the exact levels of service that the wealthiest families in the world achieve using the Single Family Office model.

Chapter 21

How to Move Forward

After learning about the discovery and stress testing I conduct with new clients, many business owners ask whether we offer stand-alone discovery and stress testing services. While that might be somewhat valuable, offering stand-alone services like those would be inconsistent with the values on which my DiNuzzo Middle-Market Family Office™ operates and the value-driven approach I take with respect to my fees.

As to the values on which my DMMFO operates, the real impact my team and I make does not come from any single activity we perform but the combination of all we do. Thus, isolated discovery or stress testing might reveal issues that could be addressed, but those services alone won't solve any real problems for the client. Helping the client choose among possible solutions to the problems is what moves the needle.

Moreover, a piecemeal approach rarely works even when someone approaches me to help with specific services like exit planning or risk management. In those cases, I often learn through discovery that they don't actually need the specific service they came to me requesting. They were pitched exit planning or risk management services by some piecemeal professional looking to sell them services. That professional told them they needed exit planning, and they're doing their due diligence to shop around. But after talking with them about their goals for 30 minutes, I often discover that they really don't need the service they thought they did or that they do need the service but need something else first. The other professionals were just trying to sell them the only product or service they sell.

With exit planning, in particular, business leaders often think they need exit planning but really need succession planning because they want to pass their business to their children, not sell it to a third party. Others come for succession planning but really need exit planning because nobody in their family wants to inherit the business. Again, they don't know what they don't know. They just know what a professional who has only one or two products to sell is telling them they need—because that's all they sell. We conduct discovery and stress testing to identify the right options. We don't conduct discovery and stress testing to lead clients in one predetermined direction.

As to my fees, charging for discovery or stress testing would run counter to how I approach client service. I only charge fees when we provide solutions to clients, not when I identify gaps or opportunities. Unlike some other Private Wealth Advisors, I don't charge for discovery or stress testing. If you believe working with the DMMFO would be a good fit for you, there's no reason for me to charge you for discovery or stress testing. If you're a good fit for DMMFO, you'll get that for free and only pay a fee if we find high-impact solutions to fill gaps or find opportunities to help you better achieve your goals.

You only pay when you choose to move forward with a recommendation. And, even then, you only pay based on value and only pay the professionals who provide that value to you. Many times, I don't make a penny—particularly with service providers I introduce you to who work best when contracting directly with you, such as many of the healthcare and biohacking options I can connect you with, or when the solution you choose doesn't require my services to implement, such as acquiring certain insurance policies. It doesn't matter.

And unlike most professionals, I'm not bashful about discussing fees with clients and don't hide my fees from my clients when presenting options to them. Because of the way my fees are structured, any fees my clients pay are so *inconsequential* when compared to the value they receive in return, my clients don't think twice about fees.

Additionally, DMMFO clients only get the services they choose. If a client has no interest in certain solutions, such as upgrading to an Executive Health Physical Plan, we don't force it on them. And my clients don't incur any charges just because a product, service, or professional is technically available to them from my team of specialists. They only pay for the products or services they choose to move forward with and only when they move forward.

Moreover, if you are already working with professionals who are serving you well, I work *with* those professionals to support, complement, and supplement what they are already doing for you. My goal is to get you the best care and support possible. I don't force anything on you.

Together, this approach is what makes the DMMFO experience work so well for my clients and their existing trusted professionals. It's how my team and I change my clients' lives for the better. It's how they can finally get to focus on operating their businesses and living their best lives. A piecemeal approach doesn't have the same impact on their lives, even when it's done by specialists like those on my cohesive team of specialists.

The holistic approach to helping clients achieve their business, family, philanthropic, and other goals is what changes clients' lives. To begin to experience that customized, holistic approach for yourself, visit DiNuzzo-FamilyOffice.com.

 Keys to Chapter

- As to the values on which my DiNuzzo Middle-Market Family Office operates, the real impact my team and I make does not come from any single activity we perform but the combination of all we do. Thus, isolated discovery or stress testing might reveal issues that could be addressed, but those services alone won't solve any problems for the client.

- A piecemeal approach rarely works even when someone approaches me to help with specific services like exit planning or risk management. In those cases, I often learn through discovery that they don't actually need the specific service they came to me requesting.

- You only pay a fee when you choose to move forward with a recommendation—you don't pay for the discovery process. And, even then, you only pay based on value, and only pay the professionals who provide that value to you. Many times, that means I don't make a penny—particularly with service providers I introduce you to who don't require my continued expertise and support, such as many of the healthcare and biohacking options I can connect you with.

- Moreover, if you are already working with professionals who are serving you well, we work together with those professionals to complement and supplement what they are already doing for you.

- To begin to experience that customized, holistic approach for yourself, visit DiNuzzoFamilyOffice.com.

Conclusion and Invitation

The journey of a thousand miles begins with a single step.—**Lao Tzu**

I f I can show you one thing that none of your current advisors have brought to your attention, would you be interested?

And if I could work solely with you on just that one issue without impacting anything your current advisors are doing, would you be comfortable with that?

I designed my DiNuzzo Middle-Market Family Office™ to be flexible enough that our relationship can grow together from a single service to the full benefits you learned about in this book, and more.

That's what the discovery process is all about …

Take taxes, for example.

Taxes are going up and look like they'll do nothing but go up for the foreseeable future.

What are you doing to save taxes?

If I could show you a methodology to save taxes, is that something you would be interested in?

Or take any other of the benefits we help middle-market business owners achieve …

If I could show you how to increase cash flow, what could that do for your business or life?

If I could show you how to protect your assets from lawsuits, would that be something you would want to learn about?

If I could show you how to have a well-coordinated team of experts analogous to a Single Family Office whose sole focus will be to work seamlessly to help you achieve your business, family, financial, philanthropic, and healthcare goals, would you want to learn more?

And if I told you that you could have all this available at your fingertips without having to worry about being billed every time your professionals read an email or think about you, would that sound like an arrangement that would benefit you?

I can.

I can do all that, and more, all while working well with your existing advisors and coordinating to bring the appropriate specialists from my team, as necessary, to supplement and complement what they do for you to provide the level of service you need and deserve.

If you are worth $10 million or more …

If you generate more than $10 million in annual revenue in a business you own …

If you make more than $1 million a year …

Or if you're well on your way to any of those three targets …

I have a solution you cannot afford to ignore.

So if you're sick of people always trying to sell you whatever makes them the most money and instead want to invest in understanding your and your family's biggest goals and then pulling together a team of experts to help you achieve those goals, my DMMFO is that solution.

I built it for you to …

improve your business operations …

help you spend more quality time with people you love …

help you maximize your physical and mental wellness …

help you take care of your spouse, partner, children, grandchildren, and other family members as well as possible …

help you live your life how you want to, when you want to, the way you deserve …

grow your revenue …

reduce your risk …

save money on taxes ...

improve your sleep ...

increase your foundation of health ...support others ...

and achieve *all your* goals across *all* aspects of your life.

If you want to learn more, give me a call.

In just *20* minutes, on the phone or on Zoom, we can discuss your goals and whether the DiNuzzo Middle-Market Family Office might be the right solution for you.

You can reach me at 877.728.6564.

Or just visit DiNuzzoFamilyOffice.com to schedule a Zoom call with me and learn more about whether my DiNuzzo Middle-Market Family Office is a good fit for you.

Important Disclosure Information

Patrick J. DiNuzzo, CPA, PFS™, MBA, MSTx is the Founder, President, and Lead Consultant at DiNuzzo Middle-Market Family Office™ ("DMMFO") and DiNuzzo Wealth Management ("DWM"), an investment adviser registered with the United States Securities and Exchange Commission, located in Beaver, PA and Pittsburgh.

The book content is for information purposes only, and does not provide any personalized advice from the author to the reader that is based upon the reader's specific situation or objectives. To the contrary, no reader should assume that this book serves as the receipt of, or a substitute for, personalized advice from the investment and/or other professionals of his/her choosing.

Please remember that different types of investments involve varying degrees of risk. Therefore, it should not be assumed that future performance of any specific investment or investment strategy (including the investments and/or investment strategies referenced and/or recommended in the book), or any non-investment related content (including financial planning topics), will be profitable, equal any historical performance levels, be suitable for a reader's individual situation, or prove correct.

Certain portions of the book may reflect positions and/or recommendations as of a specific prior date, and may no longer be reflective of current positions, recommendations, or laws. Please Note: Limitations. Neither rankings and/or recognitions by unaffiliated rating services, publications, media, or other organizations, nor the achievement of any professional designation, certification, degree, or license, membership in any professional organization, or any amount of prior experience or success, should be construed by a client or prospective client as a guarantee that he/she will experience a certain level of results if DMMFO and/or DWM is engaged, or continues to be engaged, to provide investment advisory services. Rankings published by magazines, and others, generally base their selections exclusively on information prepared and/or submitted by the recognized adviser. Rankings are generally limited to participating advisers (participation criteria/methodology available at www.dinuzzo. com). No ranking or recognition should be construed as a current or past endorsement of DMMFO and/or DWM by any of its clients.

About the Author

P. J. DiNuzzo, Founder, President, Lead Consultant, Chief Investment Officer (CIO), Chief Compliance Officer (CCO), and Director of Business Development for DiNuzzo Private Wealth, Inc./DiNuzzo Middle-Market Family Office™/DiNuzzo Wealth Management, which has operated as an SEC Registered Investment Advisory Firm since 1989 and currently manages $929 million in Assets Under Management as of December 31, 2021. P. J. has devoted his entire professional career to indexing/efficient market theory, retirement planning, and educating the public regarding their benefits. He was approved as one of the first 100 Advisors in the United States with Index Research/Development Leader and Institutional Mutual Fund Manager, Dimensional Fund Advisors (DFA) in the early 1990s. DiNuzzo Private Wealth, Inc./DiNuzzo Middle-Market Family Office/DiNuzzo Wealth Management was one of the first few hundred fee-only firms in the U.S. in the late 1980s and has been consistently ranked as one of the top 500 firms in the country by multiple national publications. Under P. J.'s leadership, DiNuzzo Private Wealth, Inc./DiNuzzo Family Office/DiNuzzo Wealth Management, on numerous occasions, has been recognized as one of the "Best Places to Work" and was awarded the honor of "#1 Best Place to Work" in Western Pennsylvania/Pittsburgh in 2008, 2013, and 2016 by the *Pittsburgh Business Times*. Additionally, P. J. has been awarded the prestigious multiyear designation as a Five Star Wealth Manager. The award is given to Wealth Managers in Pittsburgh and across the U.S. who satisfy key client criteria and score the highest in overall client satisfaction.

P. J. has earned the distinguished Personal Financial Specialist (PFS™) designation. The American Institute of Certified Public Accountants (AICPA), a national professional organization of CPA professionals grants the PFS credential only to certified public accountants with a significant personal financial planning education and experience. Candidates must meet six necessary requirements including an arduous technical exam and a peer review of their ability to demonstrate significant experience in a wide range of comprehensive personal financial planning disciplines.

P. J. has been interviewed on numerous occasions regarding Middle-Market Family Offices, Closely Held Businesses, High Net Worth Individuals, Strategic Asset Allocation, Portfolio Diversification, Indexing, Rebalancing, and Retirement Income Planning on various Television and Radio programs including: *Private Wealth Magazine* with Russ Alan Prince, *Oprah & Friends* with Jean Chatzky on XM Radio, *Power Lunch* on CNBC, KDKA-TV2's *Sunday Business Page* with Jon Delano, *The Lange Money Hour* radio show with Jim Lange, ABC TV9 WCPO.com, and The Street.com TV.

P. J. has also been interviewed and quoted on a number of occasions regarding Strategic Asset Allocation, Portfolio Diversification, Indexing, Rebalancing, and Retirement Income Planning in various national, regional, and local magazines including *Kiplinger's Personal Finance* Retirement Planning, MarketWatch from Dow Jones, *Morningstar, SmartMoney, BusinessWeek, Investment Advisor, Financial Planning, NAPFA Advisor*, the *Wall Street Transcript, Wealth Management Exchange, Wealth Manager, Bottom Line Personal, InvestmentNews, Financial Advisor*, and IARFC's the *Register*.

He has also been interviewed and quoted on numerous occasions regarding Strategic Asset Allocation, Portfolio Diversification, Indexing, Rebalancing, and Retirement Income Planning in various national, regional, and local newspapers and websites including the *Wall Street Journal, Barron's*,

Reuters, Bankrate.com, CBS News, YAHOO! Finance, *Pittsburgh Post-Gazette*, U.S. News & World Report, MSN Money, *Chicago Sun-Times*, FT.com *Financial Times*, SmartMoneySelect.com, the *Atlanta Journal-Constitution*, *St. Louis Post-Dispatch*, Chicago Board Options Exchange, *Pittsburgh Business Times*, the *Sharon Herald*, the *Christian Science Monitor*, the *Beaver County Times*, *Pittsburgh Tribune-Review*, MutualFundWire.com, *Gulf News*, TMC.net, Comcast.net Finance, Rydex Investments, FreeRealTime.com, Individual.com, Lockheed Federal Credit Union, Invest 'n Retire, ABC TV9's WCPO.com, *Fort Worth Star-Telegram*, KYPost.com, Jim Prevor's *Perishable Pundit*, *Reading Eagle*, the *Toledo Blade*, Horsesmouth, DemocraticUnderground.com, the Community Investment Network, *Daily Herald*, Scripps News, the *Modesto Bee*, Hitched, Prime, *El Paso Times*, Paladin Advisor, Advisor Max, Denverpost.com, Oswego Daily News, The Dollar Stretcher, the *Ledger*, the *Columbus Dispatch*, *Savannah Morning News*, and Hampton Roads News Channel.

P. J. is a member of the Financial Planning Association (FPA), the Family Office Club, the Estate Planning Council (EPC) of Pittsburgh, the American Institute of Certified Public Accountants (AICPA), and the Pennsylvania Institute of Certified Public Accountants (PICPA), the AICPA's National CPA Financial Planning Insights Panel, the National Association of Tax Professionals (NATP), the Financial Educators Network (FEN), and the Pittsburgh Society of Investment Professionals (PSIP).

P. J. chose football in lieu of a Major League Baseball offer from the Houston Astros to play with their Class A Team, as he attended and played football at Indiana University under Head Coach Lee Corso in the "Big Ten" (Bloomington, Indiana) and also at the University of Pittsburgh under Head Coach Jackie Sherrill. He later received his Bachelor of Science in Business Administration from Geneva College in Beaver Falls, PA. His graduate studies culminated in a Master of Business Administration (MBA) from the Katz Graduate School of Business at the University of Pittsburgh and a Master of Science in Tax Law (MSTx) from Robert Morris University at the downtown Pittsburgh campus. P. J. received his Certified Public Accountant (CPA) designation from the State of Delaware.

P. J. was a member of the Investment Committee on the Endowment Board for Valley Care Associates, a nonprofit organization providing adult day care, home safety consulting, and physical modifications for the elderly in Allegheny and Beaver Counties. He serves as a Finance Council Board Member for St. Blaise Church and is a member of the Department of Finance Advisory Board for Robert Morris University. He is a volunteer for and supports Habitat for Humanity and the Red Door Program for the homeless, and he is committed to his churches in Midland and Pittsburgh's South Side. He serves on the Board of Directors and volunteers for Hope House and The Center, both of which are located in Midland, PA, and support the women and youth of the community. He is a lifelong resident of the Pittsburgh and Western Pennsylvania area. He devoted over 12 years to helping and assisting numerous young men in Pittsburgh's inner city and surrounding areas by supporting and coaching over 1,000 basketball games at the Amateur Athletic Union (AAU), elementary, middle school, junior high, and high school levels attempting to teach and instill in them teamwork, trust, structure, discipline, and hard work.

A free ebook edition is available with the purchase of this book.

To claim your free ebook edition:

1. Visit MorganJamesBOGO.com
2. Sign your name CLEARLY in the space
3. Complete the form and submit a photo of the entire copyright page
4. You or your friend can download the ebook to your preferred device

Morgan James BOGO™

A **FREE** ebook edition is available for you or a friend with the purchase of this print book.

CLEARLY SIGN YOUR NAME ABOVE

Instructions to claim your free ebook edition:
1. Visit MorganJamesBOGO.com
2. Sign your name CLEARLY in the space above
3. Complete the form and submit a photo of this entire page
4. You or your friend can download the ebook to your preferred device

Print & Digital Together Forever.

Snap a photo   Free ebook   Read anywhere